THE COSMIC GAME OF
SNAKES AND **ARROWS**

THE COSMIC GAME OF **SNAKES** AND **ARROWS**

An Oracle for Mapping Your Destiny

POLINA RUD

Destiny Books
Rochester, Vermont

Destiny Books
One Park Street
Rochester, Vermont 05767
www.DestinyBooks.com

Destiny Books is a division of Inner Traditions International

Cataloging-in-Publication Data for this title is available from the Library of Congress

ISBN 979-8-88850-221-1 (print)

Printed and bound in India by Replika Press Pvt. Ltd.

10 9 8 7 6 5 4 3 2 1

Text design by Virginia Scott Bowman and layout by Kenleigh Manseau
This book was typeset in Garamond Premier Pro with Bebas Neue, Frutiger LT Std, and Gill Sans MT Pro used as display typefaces.
Game board artwork by Polina Rud and Jónatan Schutz

To send correspondence to the author of this book, mail a first-class letter to the author c/o Inner Traditions, One Park Street, Rochester, VT 05767, and we will forward the communication, or contact the author directly at **polinarud.com**.

CONTENTS

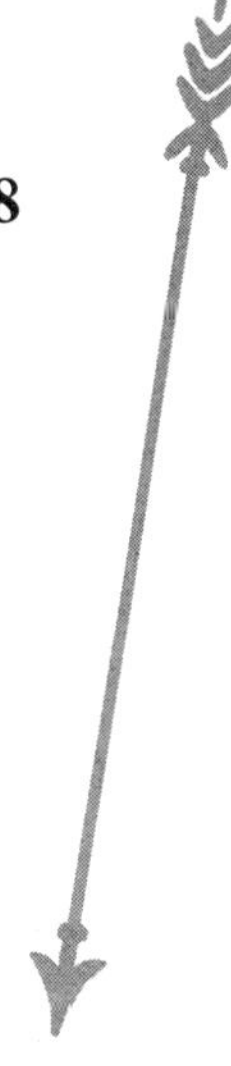

ACKNOWLEDGMENTS

People truly influence the essence of our existence, guiding us through the spectrum of emotions and experiences. Through them, we learn love and heartbreak, connection and vulnerability, and come to terms with our own identities. They serve as mirrors, reflecting both our strengths and weaknesses, shaping our journey in profound ways. Indeed, every lesson, whether gentle or harsh, is intertwined with the presence of others.

This book would have remained a mere aspiration without:

the heartfelt discussions shared within my family circle, where I explored my ideas and witnessed the echoes of their souls within me;

my grandfather, who, with his own dreams of literary pursuit, instilled in me a love for storytelling and a keen eye for detail from an early age;

my spouse, whose gentle nudges reminded me of the importance of bringing this vision to fruition;

courageous individuals who entrusted me with their stories during countless client sessions—their narratives, often richer than fiction, provided insights that even the most imaginative cinema could scarcely capture;

the remarkable encounters with artists, actors, poets, and directors, each infusing me with their unique brand of creativity and daring spirit;

the intricate interplay of fate orchestrated by the Universe, introducing dramatic twists and turns that ultimately enriched my understanding of life's complexities.

The endeavor of creating this book has taught me that life, with its myriad experiences and the people who populate it, is indeed the greatest teacher. Though it may seem as though this book bears the imprint of a single author, it is, in truth, a tapestry woven by the lives and stories of countless individuals.

HISTORY OF SNAKES AND ARROWS

Befriending Uncertainty

Where one game ends, another begins.

Jacob Schmidt-Madsen

Who hasn't played Snakes and Ladders at least once? That seemingly simple childhood game felt so profound in its stakes—one roll of the dice could send you up a ladder toward triumph or down a serpent's tail into despair. Whether competing with friends or family, we've all experienced that rush of near victory or the sting of unexpected defeat. For those cozy moments of family fun, we owe thanks to the London-based company F. H. Ayres, which brought the game to market in the late nineteenth century. But this whimsical pastime has roots far older and more intricate than its Victorian reinvention. Beneath its cheerful facade lies a history steeped in philosophy, spirituality, and cultural exchange—a story that winds like the very snakes it features.

The origins of Snakes and Ladders trace back to *gyan caupar*, or the "game of knowledge," a spiritual board game from ancient India. Designed not merely to entertain but to educate, its squares represented virtues and vices, guiding players on a metaphorical journey through life, karma, and liberation. This wasn't just play—it was a meditative tool, a representation of the cosmic order, where each roll of the dice mirrored the unpredictable hand of fate. The game, deeply embedded in Hindu, Jaina, and Buddhist traditions, encapsulated a philosophy: The path to enlightenment is fraught with obstacles, but also punctuated by moments of grace.

THE NAME OF THE GAME

The Indian game was known by different names among the religious communities that adopted and transformed it according to their beliefs. In Gujarat and Rajasthan, where the game found its earliest and widest distribution, it was referred to as *gyan caupar* by the Vaisnavas and as *gyan bazi* by the Jainas. Both names indicate a "game" (*caupar, bazi*) of "knowledge" (*gyan*), highlighting its role in offering insight into cosmology and soteriology. The earliest forms of the charts were the Vaisnava (seventy-two squares) and Jaina (eighty-four squares); these charts were associated with individual practitioners, religious institutions, and royal courts. Vaisnava charts were mostly used for religious entertainment and meditation, while Jaina charts served for religious instruction.

Interestingly, the mechanics of this spiritual journey were not entirely homegrown. European influence crept in, likely through Jesuit missionaries who brought the Italian *gioco dell'oca*—"the game of the goose"—to India in the sixteenth and seventeenth centuries.[1] Popular in Europe, this game of chance evolved from tavern gambling to a tool for moral instruction, teaching children about virtues, vices, career choices, history, and geography through a series of steps. The connection between these two games hints at a fascinating cultural exchange, where ideas flowed across continents, shaping and reshaping traditions.

The origins of gyan caupar unveil an intricate tapestry of cultural and spiritual interchanges, stretching beyond India to encompass Buddhist and Chinese traditions. Some scholars suggest its roots may trace back to a Buddhist prototype from the Pala-Sena period (eighth to twelfth centuries), whose echoes persist in Tibetan games like *sa lam rnam bzhag* ("ascending the spiritual levels").[2] Attributed to the eminent thirteenth-century scholar Sakya Pandita, this Tibetan game embodies the spiritual ascent central to gyan caupar. Sakya Pandita's contributions to the game of sa lam rnam bzhag reflect his unparalleled depth of scholarship, which saw Tibetan works translated into Sanskrit for the first time—a reversal of the usual flow of knowledge. However, it is unlikely that he originated the principles of the game entirely on his own. The thirteenth century was a period of vigorous cultural exchange across the region, with Mongol, Chinese, Tibetan, and Indian influences shaping new layers of collective wisdom.

The Tibetan sa lam rnam bzhag likely drew inspiration from *nagapasa* ("nagas and dice"), an Indian/Nepali precursor. This interconnectedness extends further, as nagapasa itself shows traces of Chinese Daoist and Buddhist promotion games, such as *xuanfo tu* ("the table of Buddha selection").[3] Crafted by Ming-era monk Ouyi Zhixu, these games illustrated spiritual progression through karmic squares, echoing the symbolic journey of gyan caupar.

THE GAME OF LIFE

The concept of life's path has intrigued philosophers, theologians, and pilgrims for centuries. Consider the profound wisdom of Lao Tzu, whose classic work *Tao Te Ching* begins with the words: "The Way that can be described is not the eternal Way."[4] In the realm of the game, the concept of *dharma* emerges, a sacred term among Buddhists representing the righteous path designed for thoughtful people.

The game itself reflects this principle of the human journey. It invites players to traverse the trunk and canopy of the Eternal Tree, which has grown since the dawn of time and will only disappear at the end of the world. Its top touches the heavens, while its roots plunge into the underworld, serving as a path for the gods to ascend and descend. Those who discover it ascend to godlike status, attain immortality, and gain the ability to perceive all created things throughout the Universe. Comparable structures that imply a person's spiritual ascension exist in various religions. For example, it's found in classical Judaism as Jacob's

Ladder, in Kabbalah as the Sephirot on the Tree of Life, in Islam as the Road to Paradise, and in ancient Egypt as the Royal Road.

In traditional cosmological symbolism, the horizontal dimension of space represents surface, limitation, passivity, quantity, and matter. In contrast, the vertical dimension symbolizes height, quality, infinity, redemption, and spirituality.

All religious traditions are concerned with spiritual progression, often represented as a series of steps or stages to be completed one at a time. These steps are typically depicted as a path or staircase ascending a hill, or as a ladder leading to heaven. Numerous myths tell of a connecting element—be it a tree, a vine, a rope, a spider's web, or a ladder—that bridges heaven and Earth. The same concept appears in rituals where a priest or initiate must climb a tree barehanded.[5]

Gyan caupar's game follows this logic, inheriting an analogous structure from Sakya Pandita's game: the ascending path, which serves as both a game and a moral teaching tool. It conveys the idea that good deeds bring rewards, while evil deeds bring punishment. The ultimate goal of this journey is Cosmic Consciousness, which signifies the culmination of the path. In this game, the lower squares represent vices or hellish states, while the upper squares represent spirituality and heavenly states. Arrows pull the player up, while snakes pull the player down. The symbolism in these movements dictates that individuals of virtuous deeds ascend the arrow and approach the "lotus feet of God," a term that symbolizes Lord Krishna's purity and grace. Lord Krishna's presence transcends earthly challenges, just as a lotus flower rises above the water's surface. Devotees aspire to emulate the lotus, growing gracefully amid life's adversities while maintaining spiritual purity. Thus, "lotus feet" encapsulates the essence of Krishna's celestial nature and encourages believers to strive for spiritual advancement amid life's complexities. Conversely, those who falter and commit sins (represented by the snake) face retribution and move further away from Cosmic Consciousness. This is consistent with the Hindu law of karma, which asserts that individuals are the architects of their destinies; that is why sinners can transform themselves into virtuous beings through good deeds.

The game board itself is a marvel of symbolism, intertwining layers of cosmology and embodied spirituality. Its layout resonates with the tantric and yogic traditions of mapping the subtle body, where the alignment of squares symbolizes the chakras—the energy centers along the spine. This design also mirrors broader metaphysical principles, uniting microcosm and macrocosm, as seen in the pervasive Indian notion of the body as a reflection of the cosmos. The journey through the game reflects a spiritual ascent, guiding players from the primal instincts at the root chakra to the sublime wisdom of the crown chakra. The seventy-two squares—evoking the 72,000 energy channels described in ancient texts—serve as a scaffold for lessons in morality, self-awareness, and the ultimate pursuit of liberation. These symbolic underpinnings, likely inspired by tantric charts used for meditation and visualization, reveal a transition from profound mysticism to the playful yet spiritually significant practice embodied in the game.[6]

The essence of gyan caupar lies in the pursuit of wisdom, regardless of the player's initial intent. According to the design of the game, it is the arrow of wisdom, or *jnana*, that guides one to bliss. In its classical interpretation, jnana refers to a form of yoga or disciplined action through which liberation from the cycle of *samsara*—the endless rounds of birth and rebirth—can be achieved. Yet it is more than just a path to freedom; it is a way of realizing, understanding, and drawing closer to the divine essence of creation itself.

This process aligns with the Hindu view of the world as a stage where all actions unfold under the will of the divine. As the Sanskrit epic the *Ramayana* puts it:

> Our world is a grand stage, and we are the actors in a cosmic drama. Yet, every action we take is inspired by the divine will of God, who governs both our immortal souls and mortal bodies. In this cosmic play, we are called to participate with unwavering strength and determination.

A similar perspective is echoed in the *Mahabharata*, where the world is likened to a game of dice between Siva and Parvati,[7] emphasizing the perfection and inevitability of all that transpires.

Jnana's wisdom bridges the gap between human perception and divine understanding, revealing life's intricate design as a cohesive whole. By exploring the patterns of recurring tendencies in the material world, seekers could uncover the interplay between material and immaterial energies and matter. Following the path of jnana, "one ultimately realizes that there are no miracles; rather, there are varying degrees of knowledge."[8]

DICE OF DESTINY

In gyan caupar, the die plays a pivotal role, allowing the individual to discern the precision or illusory nature of their intention for the game, and to evaluate their decisions made as they move from one square to the next. In Indian culture, the philosophical concept of karma, or fate, found an unlikely mirror in dice. Yes, these small, unassuming dice of chance became vessels for the weighty ideas of destiny. The *Rigveda*, an ancient sacred text, even contains passages of prayers to the dice. In these verses, dice are not mere tools; they are almost divine beings:

> *The Heroes dressed with fire the fatted wether [sic]:*
> *the dice were thrown by way of sport and gaming.*
> *Two reach the plain amidst the heavenly waters,*
> *holy and with means of purification.*[9]
>
> *The Hymns of the Rigveda*, Book 10

The player communicates with the dice, seeing them as having answered their prayers and as messengers of higher powers. Dice are the "sons" of the Great Vibhadaca, the one who weaves the threads of fortune. They possess a unique power: They bridge the connection between the player's soul and their destiny, literally holding the strings of their lives.

The use of dice to introduce randomness into games is not unique to India. It's a practice that echoes throughout human history and geography. From the Germans to the North American Indians, Maya, Aztecs, Inuits, Africans, and various Asian civilizations, these tiny objects have played a role in necromancy, divination, and games of chance. They bring an element of the unknown to the table, ensuring that victory isn't just about calculated plans, but also about reactions, choices, and taking the leap into uncertainty.

Throughout life's journey, the pervasive fear of uncertainty often grips individuals, forcing them to relentlessly pursue a sense of security at all costs. This relentless pursuit leads to the sacrifice of one's true desires, one's purpose in life, and sometimes even one's health. People are willing to sacrifice everything on the metaphorical altar of imagined security and safety.

However, within the realm of the gyan caupar game, individuals are given the opportunity to confront the enigmatic, effectively allowing them to refine their relationship with the unknown. It serves as a platform for practicing how to approach the unfamiliar, cultivating neural pathways that foster a sense of ease and trust in the face of uncertainty. The game serves as a pedagogical tool, much as young animals and children learn important life skills through playful activities that will serve them well in their adult lives.

Participants of gyan caupar weren't solely driven by the desire to win or lose; instead, they embarked on a quest to decode the enigmatic aspects of their fate, essentially entering into playful dialogues with the divine. When we extend this concept to a broader spectrum, we recognize that it wasn't only individual random elements that were at play but also a board game that acted as a channel for divine intentions. A fortuitous dice roll or a triumphant game was a symbolic reflection of a prosperous life, in harmony with the gods' wishes.

In the ancient and analogical worldview, the entire cosmos was a tightly woven tapestry, indicating that nothing unfolded by pure chance or randomness. Each event held a specific purpose and meaning within the grand design orchestrated by the divine. In the classical-traditional perspective, the very concept of randomness, as we perceive it, simply did not exist. Instead, it was seen as destiny or the will of a higher power. Aristotle himself articulated that "probable is that which happens often," underscoring the importance of the frequency of events.[10] For the Chinese, embracing the inherent chaos of nature, replete with its "strange attractors," helped them decipher the underlying order amid certain occurrences. Randomness was not dismissed as a mere accident but was understood as the harmonious alignment of events within a favorable context.

Gyan caupar evolved over the centuries, adapting to the beliefs and practices of different religious communities. We have already mentioned two examples of this: In Jainism it became *gyan bazi*, a tool for teaching cosmology, and among the Vaisnavas, it served as entertainment with a spiritual twist. Across India, during festivals like Vaikunth Ekadasior Mahasivratri, the game has taken on ritual significance, a playful reminder of life's impermanence and the pursuit of higher truths. Both festivals are observed over the course of a single day and involve staying awake through the night in praise of either Visnu (Vaikunth Ekadasi) or Siva (Mahasivratri). Today, approximately 150 original game boards are known to exist worldwide. No longer used for gameplay, these boards have transformed into objects of contemplation. Most were discovered in regions such as Nepal, Tibet, Mongolia, India, Pakistan, and Iran, dating back to approximately the eighteenth century. While the names differ,* the fundamental essence remains the same—a game of wisdom, a game of knowledge, and a game of liberation.

*Some of the names and their translations are *gyan chauper* ("the game of wisdom/knowledge/gnosis"), *jnana bazi* or *gyan bazi* ("the game of knowledge"), *vaikunthapaali* or *paramapada sopanam* ("the ladder to salvation"), *moksha patam* ("ups and downs"), *shatranj-al-arifin* ("chess of the wise"), and *nagapasa* ("the noose of serpents").

THE GAME OF SELF-KNOWLEDGE

The version of gyan caupar published by Indian philosopher Harish Johari in 1975—*Leela, the Game of Self-Knowledge*—introduced significant reinterpretations. He referred to the game as Leela, reshaping the traditional boards to align with contemporary understandings while retaining their spiritual essence. Johari's work draws on a copy preserved by the family of a commentator from Uttar Pradesh, dating back roughly 150 years. As for the interpretation of the game's squares, Johari mentions that the board was originally accompanied by a book of chants called *schlokas*.[11] With each roll of the dice, players would chant the mantra for the square they landed on. These shlokas described the nature and meaning of the space, infusing each roll of the dice with spiritual and philosophical significance.

Sadly, the book of chants has been lost, and it is now customary to provide written commentaries to illuminate the game's meanings. These interpretations, however, are never static—they shift with the philosophical, religious, and historical contexts of their time, ensuring the game's relevance to each new generation. This fluidity is precisely why I initially considered titling the book *The Cosmic Game of Snakes and Arrows for the New Era*, as a nod to the fresh layers of meaning it continues to acquire.

The book follows the structure of the game as presented by Johari, including the names of the squares and the fundamental logic of the board. However, the commentary for each square integrates modern philosophy, contemporary psychological approaches, and spiritual perspectives, aiming to uncover and articulate insights that make this divine oracle more accessible to a broader audience. The game itself remains alive and continues to evolve under the guidance of its teachers and masters. As history has shown, the game speaks through the conceptual languages of various traditions and, I believe, transcends any single philosophical or psychological framework.

The evolving commentaries act as a mirror of their age, reflecting contemporary language and ideas while staying rooted in the paradigms of the era. For the Vaisnavas, it held one set of meanings; for Buddhists, another. And for you, perhaps, it will mean something entirely your own. This adaptability underscores the living nature of gyan caupar. With each reinterpretation, it bridges the timeless pursuit of wisdom and liberation with the conceptual languages of different philosophies and schools, continually weaving new meanings into its enduring framework. It reflects a truth larger than any single philosophical or psychological school. This interplay reveals the enduring universality of the human journey—a shared odyssey of trials, growth, and transcendence, vividly mirrored in the medium of this living board game.

GYAN CAUPAR AND MY JOURNEY THROUGH GRIEF

My very first existential question surfaced while sitting on the bed in my childhood bedroom. I was five, and it was an evening like any other, with my parents engrossed in the evening news. I found myself absent-mindedly drawing autumn leaves on the wallpaper. Then, out of nowhere, a weighty question pierced my mind: What if my parents were no longer here? I can still feel the tears that welled up when I realized this possibility, and it's the only scene from my early years that my memory can spontaneously conjure up. It was my first encounter with the concept of death.

While my school friends were immersed in the works of Carlos Castaneda, I stumbled upon Lobsang Rampa's book *The Third Eye* while exploring the dusty shelves of my grandfather's library one summer. It wasn't the book's title that initially piqued my interest; at the tender age of ten, I had little inclination toward spiritual matters. My primary motivation was that I had exhausted my supply of detective novels and was eager to dive into another book. In those days, we didn't have internet access at home, and the not-so-quiet atmosphere of 1990s Russia would not have allowed me to go to the bookstore alone.

The book's detailed descriptions of Buddhist funeral traditions fascinated me even more than the novels of Gilbert Chesterton and Agatha Christie. Phrases like "the disposers of the dead who chop up corpses and feed them to vultures" made a deep impression on me. Little did I know then that life was gently and meticulously preparing me for important lessons by orchestrating a series of encounters with death.

RECONCILING WITH DEATH

When I was seventeen, I faced death for the first time. On the day of my high school graduation, my first boyfriend, my first love, was tragically struck by a car. It was one thing to read about the rituals and beliefs surrounding death in various cultures, but to see the lifeless body of someone I loved was an entirely different experience. I was completely disoriented, as if a heavy weight had crushed me, leaving me with impaired vision and hearing.

The next day I had to sit for the university entrance exams, which turned out to be the easiest exams of my life because I no longer cared about success. Strangely enough, I excelled in all the exams and secured a scholarship to a prestigious university. Then I arrived at a mistaken belief that I would grapple with for a long time afterward: Great success comes at a high price.

As the exams drew to a close, I cried incessantly, unable to eat or drink, and struggled with the relentless onslaught of suicidal thoughts, exacerbated by the towering windows of my twenty-third floor apartment. It felt like there was only one way out. However, there was a huge bookcase near those windows, and in a moment of overwhelming emptiness and intrusive melancholic memories, my eyes fell on the *Encyclopedia of World Religions* with a bookmark in the "History of Buddhism" chapter.

I couldn't be sure if I had ever read this book before; perhaps I had only prepared a school presentation on it. Yet the bookmark was there. It may sound like a sentimental story, but that book literally saved my life. It was during this time that I began to realize that grieving for loved ones is often a form of selfishness, driven by our longing for the time we once spent with them and the familiar routines they brought to our lives.

As I delved into the pages of the book, I discovered insights into the rebirth of souls, the concept of the *bardo*, and the thread that connects the soul to the body; it provided me with solace and a sense of comfort.

However, death is an experienced and profound teacher. It introduced me to a new lesson, assigned me homework, and returned to evaluate the completed assignments. The following year, around the same time, my grandmother, with whom I shared a close relationship, passed away. The grief was overwhelming, the pain just as sharp, but this time, those suicidal thoughts no longer surfaced.

I continued to read, delving into topics such as the absence of death and the liberation of the soul. Although the analogy of the body as a prison and worn-out clothes made sense intellectually, my heart couldn't quite grasp it. During one of my deep meditations, however, I had a profound experience. I saw my own death—my soul leaving the body with immense joy, dancing and shedding the old form as if it were a repulsive burden, exclaiming, "Finally, it's over." Not only was I surprised, but it was a moment of realization that highlighted the disparity between information and true knowledge that gyan caupar's square 45, Accurate Knowledge, touches upon.

Over the next two years, I attended the funerals of two more loved ones and began to associate spring with death. For some reason, the people I was close to died in the spring when nature was reborn, and their souls underwent a similar transformation. In these moments my mind often traveled to Lhasa, to the mountains where countless bodies were laid to rest, where death was embraced as a joyful transition, and where the body was seen not more than as a vessel for the soul. In these mountains, people played the Tibetan game of liberation.

I discovered this in a rather unconventional way. During those four years, I was not only an avid reader, but I also ventured to explore some of the most peculiar places associated with Eastern cultures. Such places were relatively rare in those days compared to what you can find today. In the heart of Moscow, I came across a place where the most authentic tea ceremonies took place. Guests were required to remove their shoes before entering rooms decorated with exquisite screens with intricate oriental patterns. They would then sit on the carpeted floor, cushioned by the softest pillows imaginable.

The room was crowded, but the only available seat was in the back corner. I plopped down on my pillow hoping to write the essay assigned at the university, but behind the screen there was a loud conversation, first in an unknown language, and then suddenly a parallel translation into Russian began. As I found out later, two scientists from India, who were in Moscow for a scientific conference at the Institute of Oriental Studies, were engrossed in a discussion about a strange game.

Later they presented me a book that offered interpretations of the game's squares. One concept that was frequently emphasized was the idea that death could be viewed as a profound "transition to a higher plane," in which the departed soul ascends to heaven by means of a ladder or rope.

As I immersed myself in mastering this game and unraveling the connections between its squares, I was on the verge of a fifth encounter with death, for spring was approaching. However, by what I believe to be coincidence, this encounter did not occur. In my psyche, however, the game became strongly associated with the completion of a series of losses of loved ones. During the summer, I first encountered gyan caupar while preparing for a university exam on world religions. Once again, fate played a role: My preparation required extensive reading of various foreign articles and books related to religion. In the university library, I downloaded over fifty diverse sources. When I got home, I realized that Johari's book *Leela, the Game of Self-Knowledge* had somehow made its way into my download list. My exam success was suddenly in jeopardy.

I spent entire days playing the game, trying to grasp its intricate concepts. Sometimes the reasons why I kept landing on the same squares eluded me, and the connections between them were not always obvious. As a result, I began to explore all the states proposed by the game through various philosophical and psychological paradigms. In order to dissect my own psyche based on these theories, I developed exercises and questions for myself, many of which are included in this book. Here

I've compiled all the insights I've personally experienced, those I found valuable, and—most importantly—those that brought relief.

REALIZATIONS, INSPIRATIONS, AND GROWTH

As a result of several exercises, especially those related to identifying secondary benefits (see p. 32), and deep meditation with the mantra *Om,* I came to understand why I was repeatedly descending the snake of darkness in the game. I realized that my entire psyche revolved around a single question: What would my mother say? This idea reminded me of a scene in the animated film *Inside Out* where different emotions were in control, and there I had a figurative mother who guided all my decisions. It was a hidden mechanism of my psyche, much like a computer virus that hides because it does not want to be deleted. Although I rarely sought my mother's advice, her values influenced every decision I made. As a result, my existence was constructed from my mother's perspective, and in a spiritual sense, I had not yet truly lived.

As a result, I struggled to find my purpose and constantly felt inadequate, as if my skills were insufficient. The result was an overwhelming sense of insecurity, both within myself and about my future. To address this, I embarked on a special journey, turning to various forms of divination such as astrology, runes, tarot cards, and other oracles. I enrolled in courses, studied fervently, and constantly sought answers. I immersed myself in almost every modern oracle, yearning for certainty and assurance that everything would turn out well, that my life had meaning. Several times a day I turned to tarot cards or runes to find answers to even the simplest, most mundane questions.

Meanwhile, gyan caupar kept sending me to square 24, Bad Company, every game. At first, I couldn't understand what this meant—there were no malicious people surrounding me. However, it became clear that the runes and cards had clouded my mind and completely atrophied this spiritual "muscle" called intuition. Gyan caupar gradually weaned me from my reliance on oracles, rekindled my ability to feel, and, most importantly, taught me that certainty stifles adventure and encourages stagnation. The safest path is not one of predictability or control, but one that makes room for the divine, the Universe, or higher powers. To relinquish control is to unburden oneself and entrust the heavens to their rightful guardian—God.

Bringing the concept of higher powers back into my worldview wasn't an easy process; it took years. But with each game, gyan caupar persistently demonstrated that the world operates under a deep sense of fairness. It explained the true reasons behind seemingly unfair events, revealing the intricate cause-and-effect relationships that at first seemed undeserved for me or my loved ones. Gradually, the concept of karma unfolded for me. It became clear that sometimes the roots of what happens in this life may lie not in psychological patterns, but in the actions of past lives.

My understanding deepened as I immersed myself in the psycho-archetypal method. Within the framework of the psycho-archetypal map, there exists a zone known as the *karmic tail.* This is the reservoir of experiences that we carry with us into our present incarnation, whether they originate from our past lives or from experiences in parallel realities. If we consider the theory of quantum entanglement, which earned the Nobel Prize in 2022, or draw parallels with the film *Everything Everywhere All at Once,* inspired by this theory, it's plausible to entertain the idea of parallel lives. Nevertheless, our primary focus here is not on delving into the intricacies of physics or philosophy, but rather on understanding the tangible impact of these past experiences on our current incarnation. At the time of writing this book, I have conducted about two hundred consultations, and it is notable that not a single person's past life failed to align with the challenges they currently face. This realization underscores the concept of universal justice.

The difficulty in grasping this concept stems from the limited perspective we have. Our perceptions are clouded by numerous blind spots that prevent us from seeing the bigger picture. However, once the awareness of universal justice becomes part of your worldview, higher powers, whether you call them God or some other name, seem to fall into their rightful place. It's as if, through this realization, we express gratitude to the Creator for life's most challenging scenarios, indicating our acceptance of the universal plan. We stop fighting the Creator and trying to rewrite the Great Director's script according to our "fair" standards. I came to understand that continuing to fight God, trying to convince him that I shouldn't meet death, that I don't deserve it, or other similar notions, would only result in more suffering. It seemed wiser to be on the same team as God.

Reconnecting with God was incredibly challenging, especially because of the idea that my father was the cause of my parents' divorce. This connection between God and the father is a deeply ingrained aspect of those raised in societies influenced by Abrahamic religions. Whether a person identifies as a believer or an atheist, this connection persists. When I excluded my father from my worldview or treated him with contempt, I simultaneously excluded God from my life. To bring God back into my life, I had to truly understand and accept my father. This was a lesson that gyan caupar constantly reinforced by sending me to square 5, Physical Plane, to confront these aspects of my lineage.

When I mention God, I'm referring to higher powers without any allegiance to a particular religion. This lesson from gyan caupar is discussed in square 29, Blind Faith, which underscores the potential pitfalls of following commandments or laws without questioning them. Rational understanding is one thing, but personal experience is another. It feels like this is the watchword of my life—it keeps throwing up practical lessons.

Throughout my childhood, my grandmother, who is now deceased, held deep religious beliefs. As a result, I spent many of my early years near a church. And when my first love died, my father, after witnessing my suffering for several months, arranged a meeting with a priest. I was eager to discuss the profound truths I had discovered in books on Buddhism and Hinduism with a knowledgeable spiritual authority. However, the priest rebuked me for exploring other religions and considered it a grave sin. At that time, I lacked empathy and the ability to respect differing opinions, and the priest had no such ability either.

This led to a heated altercation based on arguments I believed to be correct, after which I left and didn't enter an Orthodox church again for another seven years. The game taught me the limits of blind faith.

However, as the dynamics of the game itself illustrate, states of frustration and sadness cannot persist indefinitely, and the process of learning continued. Diametrically opposite emotional states exist on adjacent squares. This might appear to be a feature confined to the game, but it's a principle that extends to life as well. Gyan caupar instructed me not to dwell in negative states, emphasizing that sadness arises when a person resists and disagrees with what has happened, essentially arguing with the divine plan. Through numerous games, I came to the realization that sadness resides in the interval between two moments of joy. Perceived in this way, it becomes more manageable for the psyche.

At the same time, I observed a longing to maintain and increase feelings of happiness. Yet it proved elusive. Happiness either became banal or led to apathy. Countless self-help books revolve around the quest for happiness, and marketing consistently promotes making people happy, inadvertently stigmatizing negative emotions. It's as if being sad or angry is considered abnormal, emotions we must quickly cast aside. Gyan caupar instructed me to decipher why these emotions exist, what they mean, and why they serve as vital markers in navigating this life. Negative states shouldn't be locked away in the depths of your subconscious; they must serve a purpose. The relentless pursuit of happiness inevitably breeds sorrow; the pendulum of emotions will continue to swing until you grow weary of this emotional teeter-totter. At the peak of the game, there is no bad or good, no distinction between joy and sorrow; everything becomes neutral—victories and defeats, highs and lows.

The exhilaration of ascending on a single arrow often leads to descending on the snake. However, a state of healthy indifference, as opposed to apathy, fosters growth and propels you forward. In my early games, I would become immensely frustrated when I encountered snakes, feeling as if I had made a mistake and was being reprimanded for it, and I would long to finish the game quickly. The more intense my desire, the more obstacles the game threw in my way. Then I realized that when I win, my game is over, and when I reach the stage of full realization, the goal we all strive for, my life will end. The desire to win, to reach a certain point of clarity and understanding, is essentially a desire for a quick death. So, I let go of that desire and began to enjoy the game, which could stretch over three days and occasionally even a full week. I took a patient approach, allowing the game to gauge my level of enjoyment throughout the process. Once gyan caupar was convinced, the games became extremely short, some as short as ten moves.

The art of enjoying the process is paramount, not only in the game, but in Buddhism as a whole. The Protestant work ethic, the foundation of capitalism, has fostered a sense of guilt about pleasure. Gyan caupar even devotes an entire square (9, Kama Loka) to teaching us how to have fun and derive pleasure, including from a sexual perspective. In Buddhism, unlike Christianity, the sexual act isn't tied solely to procreation. Sexual pleasure is one of the great pastimes of the gods.

I revisited the interpretations of the squares four times, with the first version handwritten for my personal use, to make sure I didn't forget the insights the game had provided. As I dissected each of the squares, it seemed as if life was tutoring me on how to become more immersed in what I was documenting. Remember my life motto: Understanding is one thing, living is another. My reality has dutifully adhered to this motto. Therefore, I hope my interpretations align with your experiences and assist you in understanding your psyche, possibly fostering a dialogue with death.

What will future encounters with death look like? I am certain that death will continue to find its way into our lives, even in the face of evolving technology and new psychological challenges. Gyan caupar, the greatest and wisest teacher on my journey, has guided me through countless difficult moments, and I believe it will continue to do so in the future. I'm grateful for its guidance. Although I feel fear, I also feel a willingness to move forward.

HOW TO PLAY SNAKES AND ARROWS

OVERVIEW AND OBJECTIVE

At the heart of this adventure is a mission that will lead you to square 68, Cosmic Consciousness. Upon reaching this destination, you can rest assured that in the vast tapestry of the Universe, your request has already begun to take shape. Your duty? Live the lessons learned on your journey and let the fulfillment of your dearest wish unfold.

SETUP

To engage in this game, you'll need a few essential tools: a game board, a single die, this guidebook, and a personal item or amulet infused with your energy. This personal item will serve as your representation on the playing field, underscoring its importance in this endeavor. All players begin with their personal amulet on square 68, Cosmic Consciousness.

Setting Intentions

Before starting the game, consider doing a meditation for your first chakra (*muladhara*). You can easily find a video or audio meditation for this purpose on platforms such as YouTube. This practice can help quiet the mind, tune you into the game, and connect you to your emotions and current concerns. From this emotional state, each player shapes their intention by framing it as a question or statement. The key element is to make this intention a true reflection of what you wish to experience, realize, learn, or receive. As you formulate your intention, it's important not to be influenced by other people's wishes or to judge your own. There's no need to worry about whether your request is too materialistic or not "spiritual" enough. Concern for your material well-being is intertwined with your spiritual journey, for the degree of abundance often correlates with how brilliantly you manifest your unique talents in this world. Each intention is equally important, as I've seen countless players explore new career directions, venture into uncharted realms of knowledge, seek companionship, or even master a new language. The key is to immerse yourself in your own concerns, not those of your family, spouse, children, or parents. This is the moment when a touch of selfishness can be beneficial. It's your chance to do some deep introspection and illuminate areas of your life that need clarity and order.

An advisable practice during the formation of your intention is to refrain from using the word *not*. For example, replace "I am no longer sick" with the more affirmative "I am healthy." If your intention is to bring closure to a particular chapter in your life or to accelerate a learning experience, you can use the phrase "I refuse to . . ." (e.g., "I refuse to become addicted to smoking" or "I refuse to learn difficult lessons through illness").

Interestingly, when expressing their intentions, many people often seek advice, guidance, or validation for their choices. Instead of asking, "Should I . . . ?" or "Am I making the right choice by . . . ?" try framing your inquiries as, "What is the reason?" or "What is stopping me?" This seemingly subtle shift in phrasing reveals much about your personality, decision-making tendencies, and relationship to responsibility. It's a chance to break free from age-old patterns where you may have relied on a higher power to make decisions, perhaps due to religious or societal influences. These changes over time indicate a shift in the way humanity perceives its connection to the divine, such as the shift to emphasize personal agency during the Renaissance. Despite evolving worldviews, the tendency to deflect responsibility remains, only the recipient changes from God to parents or partners. Accepting responsibility means leaving the cocoon of infantilism, where decisions were made for you by authority figures higher up the social hierarchy. It's a willingness to accept the consequences of your choices. The game, it may seem, hasn't even started yet, but you're already unraveling the intricate tapestry of your psyche. Pay close attention to these nuances; they'll make it easier to articulate your desire and help you dive into the game with clarity. So, let's remember to replace phrases like "Am I doing this right?" with more empowering inquiries like "What's the reason?" or "What's holding me back?"

Games in which players create clear, concise intentions tend to flow more smoothly and quickly. Such games often take participants on a journey through multiple cycles, offering different perspectives on their concerns. To embark on this adventure, it's best to focus on a single, well-defined intention, even as you juggle multiple issues. Depending on how these issues intertwine and how quickly you grasp the lessons that unfold, you may find yourself delving into several aspects within a single game. We'll discuss more about how these intentions come into gameplay, along with some helpful examples, in the next section.

GAMEPLAY

Once you've carefully articulated your intention, it's time to begin the game, following the steps below.

1. Place your personal amulet on square 68, Cosmic Consciousness. *All players will remain on this space until a six is rolled.*
2. Roll the die (in turn order if playing with others).
3. If you roll any number on the die other than six, read the description for the square corresponding to that number and

reformulate your question according to the hints provided. However, remain on the Cosmic Consciousness square until you roll a six.

4. If a six is rolled, your next move awaits. Move your amulet to the square 6, Moha, read its interpretations, roll the die again and move forward the number of spaces it whispers to you.
5. If you're on a roll—literally—and another six graces your play, consider it a ticket to another roll. But here's the twist. Should you roll three sixes in a row, your reels will be reset. You'll find yourself anchored to the spot where you first conjured that triad of sixes until your next turn.
6. If you roll three sixes in a row and then another number, you must return to the square on which you started your turn before counting the new number of squares.
7. And if you're blessed with four sixes in a row, it's time to take a breather. Exit the game and ponder the lessons of your last few moves. When you're ready, start the game from the beginning.
8. Repeat this process of rolling the die and moving that number of spaces. If you land on a square with an arrow or a snake, follow it where it leads. Continue until you arrive back at square 68, Cosmic Consciousness. (While making it exactly to square 68 is the goal of the game, if you wind up moving past this square on a roll, it is possible to continue the game by going through square 72; we'll discuss the specifics of this scenario on p. 25.)

But here's the trick—when you're on the Cosmic Consciousness square at the start of the game, don't get too hung up on conjuring that elusive six when you roll the die. It's a common trap, especially for the more competitive souls among us. Instead, channel your focus directly into your intention. Visualize the scenario you're exploring, feel it resonate in your being, and then roll the die. Now, if the coveted six doesn't grace your roll, that's a sign. It's time to recalibrate your intention, or perhaps even brew up a whole new one.

Consider this example: Suppose your original intention was as simple as wanting "my own country house in Oregon." However, this particular intention limits your options quite a bit. What if your dream home isn't in the countryside, but in a bustling city? It also risks excluding the idea of living with your beloved family. So tweak that intention—how about something like "My family and I are securing a home in the perfect location for us"? It opens up new horizons and ensures that your family is comfortably included.

Let me tell you an illustrative anecdote. Once, during one of my sessions, I worked with a young woman who came to me with a heartfelt desire: She wanted to find a partner and dive headfirst into the world of love. It was a dream many share, but her story had a deeper complexity. Her self-esteem was fragile, teetering on shaky ground. She was navigating life like a maze, unsure of her direction or how to embrace her authentic self. The reality? She didn't truly seek a relationship as a journey of connection or self-discovery but as an escape from herself. Her plan was to pour every part of her being into the relationship, hoping it would reveal life's greater meaning in the process.

But life—and the game we were playing—had other plans. Her initial request didn't align with her deeper needs. It was as though the Universe resisted endorsing a goal built on avoiding inner growth. Once her intention was rephrased into something more honest and transformative—"I want to fall head over heels in love with myself!"—then what happened? The very next roll of the dice landed on a six. The reason? It's refreshingly simple—when you value and honor yourself, the chances of stumbling into an unhealthy, codependent relationship dwindle to almost nothing.

Now, deciphering these intentions can be a headache when you're playing solo. That's why I recommend playing with a guide, especially in your first few games. They can help shed light on the cause-and-effect relationships, identify the issues most relevant to your current journey, and set you on the right path.

One thing to remember on this winding journey is to be mindful of your direction. The path across the board isn't a straight sprint; it's a meandering adventure. If you ever get lost, just keep an eye on the numbers etched into each square—they'll guide you in the right direction. As mentioned earlier, the goal is to reach square 68, Cosmic Consciousness. Now, if the player skips Cosmic Consciousness, they can continue their journey through the game. But *why* does this happen, you might ask? Well, there are a couple of interesting reasons. First, it's possible that the player needs to dig deeper into their investigation and explore other aspects of the problem at hand that may have been hiding in their blind spot. Second, the game has a fascinating way of addressing multiple questions within a single session. So, if you didn't quite make it to square 68, the game is suggesting that there are several facets of your life that need attention and may be serving as obstacles on your path of spiritual evolution. In other words, it's nudging you to square 72, Tamas Guna, where you will descend on the serpent to The Earth (square 51) to deal with these unresolved issues.

Continuing Past Square 68

If your journey brought you past square 68, Cosmic Consciousness, then roll the dice and make sure you land exactly on square 72. If the value on the dice exceeds the required amount, you'll stay put. For example, if you're on square 69, you can only advance by rolling one, two, or three. From square 70, you can move on a roll of one or two. From there, you will travel on the snake down to square 51, The Earth, and continue with the game.

Pay close attention to the thoughts and feelings that accompany your movement. What answers or assumptions were dancing in your mind when you finally reached square 72? Everything that unfolds after you pass square 68 is of immense significance, for it is the game's way of revealing why you must return to The Earth, what project you must embark upon, what aspects of your life you must work through, what activities you must engage in, and exactly what you must do. The answers you'll discover here are strikingly specific and directly related to the unfolding chapters of your life.

TIPS AND "TRICKS" TO NAVIGATE THE JOURNEY

To gain a deeper understanding of the game's logic and your unique journey, record your moves, thoughts, questions, and conclusions as you navigate from one square to the next. In other words, meticulously document your dialogue with the game—note your questions and the game's answers. Each square has its own interpretation, so be sure to thoroughly read the descriptions for each state you encounter and write down, not highlight, the elements that resonate most with your current situation. There are multiple layers and explanations for each square and depending on your inquiry and your mental state on game day, the game's insights may be perceived differently and emphasize entirely different aspects. Previous game experiences may inadvertently condition or limit your perception, so stay open to evolving interpretations. After all, the reason for encountering square 3, Anger, this time may be quite different from the last time you encountered it.

For each square, I offer specific tasks to aid in your progression through each state. If you find yourself revisiting the same square multiple times, it indicates that you may not have completed the task thoroughly or that you may have overlooked something. Don't rush; take your time with these tasks. They will lead you to uncover limiting thoughts, manifest psychological patterns, or illuminate areas that need your attention. Remember, there's no rush; the game can be a long process, and you're under no pressure to start and finish in a single day.

As you progress through the game, you'll inevitably come across squares with ascending arrows and descending snakes. Once you're in such a square, be sure to carefully read the comments for both the square you originally arrived at and the one you're moving to, whether ascending or descending. The descriptions for each square with snakes or arrows will guide you in determining where to go next and the significance of these transitions.

Nothing happens randomly in this game. Pay attention to your experiences, your physical sensations, the thoughts that cross your mind, and the emotions that flow through you.

"I can't wait to finish this; I want to reach square 68! But today!"

What does this impatience indicate? It indicates your desire for immediate results in every aspect of life: A project should come to fruition as soon as possible, and your efforts should bear fruit without delay. Or perhaps it suggests that you have difficulty taking breaks, switching to other activities, or simply resting. In essence, you may find yourself fixated on certain tasks, unable to let go even when fatigue sets in or you've reached a dead end.

"How many times can I land on this square? I don't know what else to realize, or what other conclusions to come to!"

This thought highlights your aversion to revisiting and reworking things. It may imply a lack of persistence or creativity—you finish a task and that's it, you're free! But sometimes revisiting a task, rethinking it, or discovering alternative solutions is crucial. This ability to rethink and reimagine can foster creative thinking, inspire new approaches to problem-solving, and lead to improvements. Consider this scenario in business: You want to increase your customer base, and your initial strategy is to lower service prices to attract more customers. However, this approach isn't producing the expected results and is actually reducing your company's revenue. What's the solution? Rethink the mission. This may mean reviewing the numbers, exploring different marketing strategies for your business, learning about the latest technology, or even hiring an expert. In the course of these activities, you may stumble upon a technology solution that streamlines your processes and enables geographic expansion. The first approach didn't work because the Universe wanted you to uncover this unique opportunity that could catapult your business growth beyond your wildest expectations. The lesson here is to never give up; always explore alternative options. There's a hidden treasure out there for you to discover.

"Here we go down again! I just got to the top!"

So, what does this thought mean? It reveals a focus on the end result and an apparent struggle with accepting the duality of this world. Let's break it down further. The strong desire to reach square 68 as quickly as possible suggests a fixation on the end goal, and perhaps a lack of interest in the adventure that is unfolding. It's as if you're racing toward cosmic consciousness, longing for a speedy arrival, but here's the rub—striving to reach the point where your full potential is realized is, in a sense, wishing for an end to your adventure. Those who are constantly longing for the point where all tasks are completed are essentially longing for an end, similar to death, because once you've completed all your tasks in this life, your adventure is over and you're basically finished.

So, what's the underlying problem? Are you just fixated on the result? Do you not find the process itself interesting or fulfilling? Maybe it's time to reevaluate the journey. Many of us say, "When I make enough money to buy a house (or car, etc.), I'll have more time to focus on other interests, like music" or "When the kids are grown, I'll prioritize self-care." This unwavering focus on the outcome may indicate that the adventure itself has lost its appeal, and you're simply going through the motions for practical reasons or out of sheer exhaustion. It may be an opportune moment to take a break and step away from the game, or any activity, and only return when you feel truly drawn to it.

Now let's delve into the concept of the duality of this world. You may have a desire for constant happiness, emotional growth, or uninterrupted success. But have you ever considered why you might need the opposite states—sadness, anger, envy, or even defeat? Here's an exercise: Write down the five benefits of the state you're in. For example, if you descended the snake of Egocentrism (square 55), and encountered Anger (square 3), think about what you wouldn't have realized without experiencing that anger. Perhaps you would not have discovered something significant without the anger. The goal is not only to understand on a rational level but also to feel why these contrasting states play an important role in your life. It's a reminder that excessive amounts of positive or negative situations can lead to distortions. Excessive joy and unbearable sorrow, though extreme, are two sides of the same coin. Both states are extremes and need balancing or compensation. In this great cosmic dance, everything in the world is essentially neutral, and the Universe is always looking for ways to restore balance, whether you're reveling in boundless joy or struggling with unending grief.

"My friend is progressing faster. I'm happy for them, but am I inferior?" Or "I'm ahead of everyone; I seem to have a much better understanding of this world. I've got it all figured out!"

Yes, these may sound like exaggerated ideas, but when you're playing with others, it can be a challenge to completely avoid such thoughts. These thoughts subtly reflect extreme states of the wretchedness-superiority spectrum. If such thoughts arise during gameplay, it means that the pendulum of your self-esteem in life may not be stable. You may find yourself swinging between self-deprecation and overconfidence. The advice here is clear: Don't compare yourself to others; avoid swinging this pendulum. Today you may feel superior, and tomorrow not so much. There will always be someone out there who's better or worse than you in various ways. As long as you measure your worth by others, whether positively or negatively, you are inadvertently denying your own uniqueness. It's as if you're comparing yourself to others and declaring, "I'm just like them, just a little better or worse."

There's a profound lesson in the cosmic game—your journey is unique and your growth is personal. Embrace your individuality and let go of the constant comparisons. You are on your own path, and it's unlike anyone else's.

In the section to come, I'll delve into the dominant archetypes of human consciousness. They're the blueprints that shape your psyche, like hidden architects of your inner world. If you ever find yourself locked out of the game for an extended period of time, don't worry. Just dive in—you may discover crucial insights that lead you to the right questions.

BASIC ARCHETYPES

Dissecting the Human Consciousness

As a general practice, I begin by creating a numerology chart for each participant before the game. In this chart, the numbers correspond to various archetypes of human consciousness. While the game itself doesn't require any prior understanding of the participants, this preliminary numerological analysis allows me to guide them more effectively during the game. It helps uncover their pain points and identify blind spots. Sometimes a person may express a desire to work on their relationships, but their numerological chart indicates that they need to focus first on self-actualization. This approach lays the groundwork for better results in their relationships later on.

The psycho-archetypal method entails a deep exploration, sometimes even demanding the creation of a comprehensive book to fully illuminate each archetype and their intricate relationships. Nonetheless, I will now explore several archetypes that prominently manifest in many individuals, often in a detrimental manner. Achieving a positive expression of these archetypes typically necessitates the guidance of a skilled therapist, who can provide an external perspective, identify causal links to negative states, and elucidate behavioral patterns that impede the activation of an archetype's strengths. It's crucial to acknowledge that simply recognizing the presence of these archetypes in one's life marks the first step toward initiating transformation.

If you see that one or more of the archetypes discussed below are influencing your life, take a moment to identify the areas in which they are manifesting. Consider the potential secondary benefits that could result from the negative expression of these archetypes. I'll use an example to illustrate how to do this. First, let's clarify what secondary benefits are. In psychoanalysis, *secondary benefits* refer to the advantages a person gains when he or she is in an unfavorable, unpleasant, or challenging situation. On the surface, this may seem beneficial, as it can provide strength to endure challenging circumstances. In reality, however, it often acts as a hindrance, discouraging the individual from seeking a quick way out of their difficulties. Consider a person with unusual symptoms who keeps changing doctors while struggling to get a definitive diagnosis. On the surface, their goal is to find a qualified specialist and get a diagnosis. Subconsciously, however, they may be prolonging the diagnostic process because they enjoy the idea that their case is unique and, therefore, that they are special.

The main difference between secondary and primary benefits is that individuals often do not realize they are receiving secondary benefits—or they may secretly desire them. Sigmund Freud first introduced this concept when he observed that some patients seemed to deliberately slow down their recovery because being a patient garnered them the maximum attention and care from their loved ones.[1] This phenomenon of secondary benefits has been most extensively studied in people with chronic illnesses. Some of these individuals may deliberately exaggerate the severity of their symptoms in order to gain additional support and attention from medical professionals or family members. There have even been cases of people deliberately harming themselves to achieve the same goal. However, this behavior is not limited to people with chronic illnesses. In any uncomfortable situation in which a person makes no attempt to escape, secondary benefits can be suspected.

Let's look at a person who has lost their job. Even if their family is reluctantly providing financial support, they may not be actively looking for a new job. Yes, their financial resources are limited, but they enjoy having control over their time and avoiding the stress of work. Similarly, fringe benefits can hinder career growth. For example, someone who excels in their current position and could have been promoted long ago may subconsciously sabotage their career advancement. This could be because they feel comfortable in their current role and are reluctant to take on new responsibilities and greater commitments. Another scenario involves people who stay in a relationship that is no longer fulfilling. They do so because ending the relationship would require a major life reorganization and adjustment to a single life status.

To identify your own secondary benefits, first identify the aspects of your life with which you're dissatisfied. Then do a simple "I benefit/I like" exercise to understand the root of the problem. For example, "I benefit/I like not being in a relationship because I don't have to share my life with anyone," "I benefit/I like not sharing my life with anyone because I can focus on self-actualization," "I benefit/I like self-actualization because it gives me independence," and so on. Ultimately, this exercise may lead to the revelation of deep-rooted issues, such as a past trauma related to excessive direction and guidance from one's mother, as in our example. This revelation may explain why the person actively avoids relationships. Therefore, I encourage you to dissect the archetypes in a similar way, analyzing the secondary benefits of their negative manifestations. This process can provide invaluable insight into the dynamics of your own life and personal growth.

THE LOVERS ARCHETYPE OR THE SIXTH ENERGY

The Lovers archetype, also known as the Sixth Energy, exerts considerable influence in shaping an individual's approach to relationships and self-esteem. When this archetype finds positive expression, it typically manifests as gregariousness and an emphasis on meaningful connections with oneself, one's partners, and the wider world.

However, it's often in these very relationships that individuals encounter their most fragile and vulnerable aspects. Those closely associated with the Lovers archetype may discover a tendency to become overly attached to others, ultimately fostering a dependency on people and their relationships. In their quest for love, approval, and validation from external sources, they earnestly seek reassurance that they are valued and that their existence has meaning.

When such validation remains elusive, the resulting suffering can be profound. In an effort to alleviate this anguish, individuals embodying the Lovers archetype may adopt a strategic posture of striving to be the ultimate source of comfort and perfection for everyone they encounter. This dynamic can lead to a constant quest for external validation, often at the expense of their own well-being, perpetuating a cycle of longing for inner balance.

The challenge posed by the Lovers archetype stems from its deep longing for recognition, love, and the pursuit of all that is beautiful and good. This archetype tends to fixate on the positive aspects of people and situations, often overlooking the negative. As a result, those who embody the Lovers archetype may present themselves as idealists, striving for perfection in every endeavor. Yet inwardly, a sense of harmony may elude them, leading to inner turmoil and disillusionment in their interactions with others.

In its negative manifestation, the Lovers archetype can make it difficult for individuals to be sincere, open, or trusting in their relationships. They may vacillate between closing their hearts, avoiding deep emotional connections, and opening their hearts to anyone and everyone, even those who do not appreciate them or take advantage of them. This tendency to idealize people often leads to disappointment when reality does not match their lofty expectations. Frequently, individuals with a strong negative manifestation of this archetype struggle with feelings of betrayal, hurt, and ongoing disappointment.

Frequent disillusionment with others can serve as an indicator of a deeper tendency to be disappointed in oneself, stemming from a relentless pursuit of perfection, a fear of making mistakes, self-blame, and the relentless cycle of disappointment. This cycle can become self-perpetuating and damaging over time.

The core essence of the Lovers archetype lies in the ability to make heartfelt decisions and follow one's heart. However, the relentless pursuit of love and approval can overshadow this innate ability, leading to constant doubt, indecision, insecurity, and a tendency to conform to the wishes of others. Those closely aligned with the Lovers archetype may feel compelled to live up to the expectations of others, making them highly sensitive to criticism. The perception of being seen as a "bad person" can have a profound effect on them, as they work tirelessly to project a positive image.

Left unchecked, this energy can lead to a perpetual state of choice agony. Those under the influence of this archetype long so intensely for a world filled with beauty and goodness that their attention becomes singularly fixated on this pursuit. They may become disinterested in everything else and, driven by their pursuit of an ideal, find themselves jumping from person to person, job to job, and project to project. They fail to settle down, remain unfaithful to their choices, and often seem to be going through the motions without real commitment. This cycle can go on indefinitely.

These constant shifts take a toll on their physical well-being. Breathing problems, irregular heart rhythms, and increased pulse rates become apparent. Emotionally, they swing back and forth on an intense pendulum—experiencing periods of euphoric positivity followed by bouts of sobbing and negative emotions.

How can you use this in creating your intention for the game?

If you've recognized that certain aspects of the Lovers archetype are manifesting in your life, addressing your dependency on others, idealization of your social circle, ceaseless quest for external approval, and the desire to please everyone should be a priority before delving into your core intention. When your life is exclusively entwined with the lives of others, it hinders your ability to embark on your unique path, because you are essentially living through the experiences of others.

For instance, if your intention is to seek a romantic relationship, the game won't guide you on where and how to find a suitable partner because it would risk perpetuating a dependent relationship. In such a scenario, the tendency to constantly conform and strive for perfection could lead you further away from your authentic self.

The fundamental task of the Lovers archetype is to cultivate self-love and self-acceptance, embracing your imperfections and learning from your mistakes. Instead of pursuing perfection, focus on living authentically and actively working on personal growth. It's crucial not to blame yourself when things don't go as planned and to treat your blunders with lightness.

Furthermore, addressing the need for external validation is essential. At times, allowing yourself to be seen as "flawed" from an outsider's perspective can be beneficial. It's important to recognize that you can't please everyone, and people will have varying opinions of you. Your task is to stay true to your path and follow your heart's guidance, even if it means not conforming to the expectations of those around you.

Unconditional love for others, free from conventions and the acceptance of their imperfections, is a significant part of the journey. Learning to forgive, reducing your demands, and avoiding attempts to change your partner are all essential steps. Cultivate a softer and more patient disposition, open your heart, and foster harmonious relationships with yourself, your partner, and the world.

If a relationship, whether it's a friendship, a romantic involvement, or a professional collaboration, doesn't bring you joy, it's advisable to consider letting it go. If someone chooses to leave your life, it may be a necessary part of releasing yourself from a painful attachment. The sooner you let go, the easier your life will become, and new relationships and opportunities will naturally flow in.

To further progress, take time to analyze the above insights and engage in a secondary benefit exercise, such as stating, "I like seeking approval from others (or being dependent on other people's needs, or any other relevant aspect from the archetype description) because . . ." This exercise can provide clarity and guide your intention for the game, enabling you to work through the revelations that have surfaced.

THE HANGED MAN ARCHETYPE OR THE TWELFTH ENERGY

The Twelfth Energy is composed of two Sixth Energies, symbolizing the archetype of double love (6 + 6; Lovers + Lovers). Those influenced by the Hanged Man archetype are inherently driven to offer assistance, serve others, and exhibit compassion, kindness, and mercy. They are dedicated to bringing more goodness into people's lives. When this archetype is positively manifested, individuals act from the heart, driven by a selfless desire to help without expecting anything in return. They are ever ready to lend a hand, provide support, and save others, even if it is not directly related to them and even if it comes at a personal cost.

Even when the Hanged Man archetype is in a positive state, individuals may find themselves grappling with the lesson of sacrifice. It is essential for those with the Twelfth Energy to recognize that assistance should only be given from a place of abundance, when they have enough for themselves, without giving away their last resources. Providing assistance to one's detriment becomes a significant provocation for the Hanged Man archetype, as individuals with active Twelfth Energy may have a tendency to embrace suffering and sacrifice.

Frequently, these individuals become embroiled in problems, endure suffering, and save others, all the while needing salvation themselves. Yet, a deeper examination reveals that they may have inadvertently caused suffering for those around them, tormenting them, creating dependence, oppressing them, disappointing them, or causing hurt.

This creates a classic victim-demon pendulum dynamic, where they switch roles as victims or tyrants in various situations.

People with a pronounced Twelfth Energy often exhibit a propensity for complaining, feeling resentful, and perpetual sorrow, constantly believing they shoulder all burdens. However, they often provoke others to mistreat them. The Hanged Man archetype may not realize when they are overstepping boundaries by offering excessive help, potentially annoying or angering others. They forcibly push others to accept their help, even when it's unwelcome. It is crucial for such individuals to shed the victim role, recognizing the importance of self-preservation and offering themselves the same care, support, and help they extend to others. The primary challenge is to learn to accept love for themselves, a task that can be immensely difficult.

If the Lovers, as discussed earlier, struggle with the idea of someone not loving them, the Hanged Man archetype has difficulty comprehending how to accept love for oneself when they are busy giving it away.

The energy of the Hanged Man implies a state of suspension or stagnation. This suspension can manifest physically through injuries, major surgeries, enforced isolation, disability, or a mental state of victimhood, sadness, and blame. This archetype tends to attach itself to those to whom they offer love, attention, and care, often becoming deeply dependent on them. This dependency can lead to manipulation, as individuals with the Hanged Man archetype may make demands and seek to control their loved ones, resisting change and getting stuck in their ways. They struggle to accept new ideas and resist letting go of the past, remaining unable to embrace change. While they can be innovative and open to change in a positive state, they become passive and inert in a negative state, often experiencing depression, chronic fatigue, and apathy.

The core objective of the Twelfth Energy is to become proficient in asserting oneself, mastering the ability to decline, and prioritizing self-care without inflicting suffering on others. This intricate interplay involves two distinct aspects: the victim and the oppressor, which are often intertwined. Suffering typically implies that someone is causing this suffering, while the absence of suffering indicates the lack of an oppressor or a lesson. This underscores the significance of recognizing victimhood, preventing it, and ceasing it altogether. It is essential to avoid actions that harm oneself, refrain from giving away one's last resources, and renounce the notion of enduring suffering or expecting repayment unless mutually agreed upon.

How can you use this in creating your intention for the game?

If you find that facets of the Hanged Man archetype are present in your life, consider making a list of the people you support. Before delving into your primary intention, take time to understand the resources and effort you are devoting to each person. Challenge yourself to articulate why each of them has the ability to handle their own situations, and consider the idea that these circumstances may have been orchestrated by the Universe or a higher power as part of their journey. Resist the temptation to rewrite life scenarios that may have a greater purpose. Refrain from trying to save the world and every individual in it. Remember the safety protocols of air travel, where you're advised to secure your own oxygen mask before assisting others in an emergency. Embrace the power of saying no when you're not inclined to get involved, and refrain from lending or borrowing money when you're in financial need. Avoid shouldering the burdens of others when you're already tired. Maintain a vigilant awareness of potential manipulative behaviors and establish clear personal boundaries.

The basic principle is to learn how to serve others without harming yourself. Once you shift your focus from external concerns to your own well-being, you can formulate the right intention for the game: What do I really want? How can I protect and nourish myself? How can I fathom the greater divine plan in the unfolding events of my life?

THE JUSTICE ARCHETYPE OR EIGHTH ENERGY

The theme of justice, as discussed on p. 16, pertains to the futility of rescuing others. In contrast to the Twelfth Energy, the Eighth Energy seeks not only to save individuals but to restore balance in the entire world. Those aligned with the Justice archetype feel a compelling need to rectify imbalances, restore equilibrium, ensure equality, elevate some and lower others, and mediate disputes and conflicts. This heightened sense of justice can lead to aggression toward those they perceive as wrongdoers.

When the Justice archetype is positively manifested, individuals remain composed, avoid unnecessary confrontations, refrain from intervening where uninvited, and maintain neutrality, recognizing that conflicts will find resolution in due time. In its negative manifestation, however, this archetype can foster a sense of self-importance, with individuals believing they possess superior knowledge and understanding of how the world operates.

Individuals with the Justice archetype often feel a profound sense of knowing what is right, sensing all, and comprehending all. They earnestly and pretentiously impart their truths to others, leading to frequent conflicts and disputes as they strive to assert their convictions. This stems from their intense desire to uphold justice, which sometimes leads them to presume godlike roles, believing they can judge, rectify, redistribute wealth, punish wrongdoers, and aid the oppressed. They engage in the battle for justice and the rights of others, which can occasionally result in personal setbacks as they get entangled in negative dynamics, attracting even more unjust situations.

The Eighth Energy tends to categorize people into good and evil, friends and enemies, which perpetuates enduring resentment. They believe that injustices must be rectified and victims defended. They also contend that they are consistently deceived, mistreated, and betrayed, often with some basis for their claims. This outlook contributes to a cycle where they gradually accumulate grievances, becoming more entrenched in their conviction that life is unfair.

Individuals with a strong Justice archetype often complain not only about people but also about life in general, sometimes holding grievances against the divine for seemingly bestowing an unjust existence upon them. Their lives tend to reinforce these beliefs, as they approach life with a sense of resentment.

In reality, the Eighth Energy doesn't primarily combat "real" injustices but rather seeks to challenge the divine, implying that God has made errors in scripting life scenarios, imparting lessons that exceed human capacities and are fundamentally inappropriate. Engaging in a battle with the divine is a futile endeavor, making the Justice archetype's life a continuous struggle. In its negative manifestation, they fail to grasp the broader picture, the karmic cause-and-effect relationships, and the divine plan. Those with Eighth Energy often perceive life as excessively harsh, leading them toward depression or aggression, as they grapple with their grievances in various ways, either quietly or vocally.

How can you use this in creating your intention for the game?

If you notice that elements of the Justice archetype are surfacing in your life, consider a preliminary step before delving into your primary intention. Make a list of at least ten situations in your life that seem deeply unjust. In an adjacent column, try to uncover the possible reasons why God may have allowed these circumstances to occur, and what positive aspects or lessons may have resulted from them. Make an effort to empathize with anyone else involved in these situations. These life events can range from extreme scenarios such as murder, serious illness, and death to more mundane situations. It's important to approach each situation with a "why" perspective rather than a "why me?"

The Eighth Energy, when immersed in its negative aspects, can resist acknowledging that these situations may have an intrinsic purpose and that they may have played a role in attracting them. Breaking out of this cycle can be challenging because the number eight, symbolizing infinity, means that these individuals tend to persistently repeat their mistakes, often failing to draw conclusions, learn, or evolve. When presented with explanations, they can become defensive, resentful, and prideful. However, I believe in your ability to take on this task.

As you begin to see cause-and-effect relationships and expand your perspective beyond your individual point of view, you will develop the ability to discern truth from falsehood. You will come to recognize the authority of a higher power within your system, regardless of your religious beliefs, and eventually gain a sense of stability.

GAME INTERPRETATION

THE COMPLETE GUIDE

LEVEL I

THE INNER LANDSCAPE

The game field encompasses seventy-two distinct states of human existence, each replete with invaluable lessons and challenges. These states intricately mirror the vast tapestry of human experiences, endowing our lives with a rich and diverse mosaic.

Within this field, we find seven distinct rows, aligned with the seven chakras, each offering its unique set of teachings. The initial row invites you to embark on a profound journey, delving into the wisdom of the first chakra. This transformative odyssey centers on the themes of self-acceptance and a deep connection with the physical world, encompassing your body, place of origin, and earthly possessions. It is an exploration of recognizing your innate right to exist and lay claim to your material world, nurturing your presence in the realm of the tangible.

Yet, this very row is also where fear finds its dwelling. Fear, a natural biological safeguard designed to shield us, can, if not comprehended fully, become a hindrance. Confronting our fears and embarking on an inner quest to understand our own inner landscape is an essential stride on the path of personal growth and self-realization.

1 Janma BIRTH

The real voyage of discovery consists not in seeking new landscapes, but in having new eyes.

MARCEL PROUST

On the plane of Birth, square 1, the human journey into incarnation unfolds. The soul embraces a new human form, and as you open your eyes for the very first time, a world unknown to you spreads out. You gaze upon it without preconceived notions or labels, observing its raw essence. The circumstances of your birth, both in time and place, set the stage for your life's path.

In this pivotal stage, we embark on three fundamental lessons:

First—accepting the vessel of your body as it is.

Second—embracing the environment, including your parents, family members, and influential adults.

Finally—acknowledging the birthplace that shapes the backdrop for your evolving identity. It was your choice; there is nobody to blame for it. Here, one must reconcile the seeming irrationality of thoughts like "What if I had been born into a different family?" or "What if my birth had occurred in a more prosperous setting or country?"

In this square, the soul learns to harmonize with its earthly vessel, as body and soul forge a connection to heed each other's needs and desires. Furthermore, the acceptance of the family into which you were born becomes crucial. Here, you cultivate respect for your roots. Failure to absorb the lessons of Birth can lead to inner conflict with your body, environment, and family, often manifesting as resentment, criticism, and complaints, ultimately leading to the state of Anger (square 3). Nonetheless, this choice aligns with your original desire to incarnate. You were born in an ideal place, under circumstances perfectly suited to the aspirations you set for yourself upon descending into the physical realm.

However, this square can also address other aspects of your life, such as your relationships, your job, and more. Here, the origins of your desires and challenges often come to light, tracing their roots back to their beginnings. When it comes to relationships, the process of Birth unveils the intricate tapestry of how connections were woven and the initial motivations that set them in motion. You might ponder on how those connections initiated, questioning if they began with a falsehood or if the driving force was to escape loneliness or uncertainty about your life's direction. It grants you the opportunity to revisit the moment you made those crucial decisions. Let's take your job as an example. What initially motivated you to embark on that career path? Was it financial gain, the promise of recognition, or the potential for career advancement?

In many cases, the path out of a situation is intertwined with its entrance. Some things in this life cannot be changed. But they can be seen differently. Resentment clouds the view but curiosity clears it. You were not thrown into this world—you arrived. Your soul said yes. And your task is not to judge the design, but to study it.

Exercise: A Fresh Beginning

1. When reviewing your past and your family, it's essential to abandon the binary notions of "good" and "bad"—and, instead, explore the lessons learned from your parents or a certain situation.
2. Think back to your childhood experiences, recognizing what you valued and what you'd like to avoid in your adult life. What are the lessons you'd prefer not to pass on to your children? What patterns do you need to break? How can you approach things differently?

3. Consider identifying five family inheritances you aim to avoid and five that you wish to carry forward. This serves as your launching point for a fresh beginning, a leap to a higher level, an opportunity to shed the old and embrace continuous growth.

ART THAT EVOKES THE SQUARE

- *Lady Bird* (2017): Written and directed by Greta Gerwig, this coming-of-age story explores the complexities of mother-daughter relationships, the search for self-definition, and the process of breaking free from familial expectations.
- "Born This Way" by Lady Gaga: This anthem celebrates self-acceptance and embracing one's identity, reflecting on the journey of accepting oneself as they are.

2 Maya ILLUSION

Embrace the glorious mess that you are.

ELIZABETH GILBERT

Everything is interconnected. I am inextricably linked with the Universe, and the Universe is a part of me. Yet, in the human experience, we must navigate the illusion of separation. This illusion gives rise to concepts like "this is me, and this is not me" or "this is mine, and this is not mine," ultimately giving birth to the ego and dualistic thinking. Hence, a further interpretation of the square's meaning is "duality," as we struggle to reconcile these self-created divisions.

Before our earthly journey begins, there exists a state devoid of time, cardinal directions, notions of good and evil, or right and wrong. Upon entering the realm of square 2, Maya, we, as human beings, accept the physical and social laws as the guiding principles of the Great Game. Here, we inherit the perspectives on life handed down by our parents, mentors, and teachers. A divide emerges between our own desires and preferences and those imposed by influential figures in our lives. Often, a person can find themselves trapped in a mental space resembling childhood, a time when they needed to conform and meet the demands of the adults around them to secure shelter, food, care, and love. Such a person becomes accustomed to seeking approval through self-betrayal, sacrificing their own needs for the sake of others. It becomes challenging to break free from this cycle because approval feels like permission to exist.

The question then arises "Why do I exist?" For many, it's to assist others and solve their problems. But when others fade from view, we're left in a kind of void, alone with ourselves. The sense of duality may disappear, leaving us with a plethora of unanswered questions. "Who am I? What are my preferences? How do I like to spend my free time? What truly excites me, and what drains my energy?"

Engaging in this internal dialogue isn't always easy to endure. The answers may not come readily, and the profound silence can be intimidating. There's no precise recipe for rediscovering one's true self, and the temptation to immerse oneself in the concerns of others occasionally arises. "I'll address all these questions soon enough," we tell ourselves, "I'm needed for other things right now." But in running from these thoughts we continue the pattern of avoidance.

The inability to make decisions can lead to a kind of inner division. In one of my sessions, there was a man who struggled to join the game for three hours; he kept rolling a two. He had recently come to terms with his attraction to men, but he was married to a woman, supporting her dream of starting a family. He hesitated to share his true feelings with her. In this complex situation, it seemed as if he could not fully be himself. It was as if a distorted version of him, like a false avatar, occupied his place. Only when he mustered the courage to write an honest letter to his spouse, read it aloud, emotionally experienced the situation, made a decision, and was prepared to face the consequences of that decision, did the game let his true self emerge.

A dualistic perspective on life may result from past traumas that have fractured the psyche into distinct parts: the healthy, the survivor, and the traumatized. Existential traumas, like sexual assault, accidents, near-death experiences, or terminal illnesses; losses such as the death or departure of a loved one, or the loss of physical abilities and future prospects; attachment-related traumas like rejection by a parent, humiliation, violence from loved ones, or infidelity; and systemic relationship traumas such as incest, familial murder, abortion, exclusion from one's family, or hidden secrets, can all contribute to a fragmented personality that avoids facing reality. To cope, the surviving self focuses on preventing traumatic memories from entering conscious awareness. This dissociation becomes an adaptive survival strategy, preventing a descent into madness. After trauma, the body serves two masters, as if two or more riders are vying for control of the same horse. Someone ensnared in this condition lives in a perpetual state of tension, channeling all their energy into upholding this dual existence, which leaves them with scant resources for a satisfying life. The body's ancient survival mechanisms are activated, including the limbic system, leading to automatic fight-or-flight responses. As a result, the person might ignore physical symptoms until they manifest as a severe illness (the *freeze* response), experience a sense of invulnerability and grandiosity (the *fight* response), or endure panic attacks and profound internal stress (the *flight* response).

Additionally, dissociation can be manifested as escapism, with individuals shifting the responsibility for solving all their problems onto "God" and "the Universe." In this scenario, a person may feel like an eternal child, expecting the world to provide everything, fostering an illusion of unconditional love from "the world." Yet, simultaneously, they remain perpetually powerless.

Maya is our perception of the world, but is it truly real? To some, the world appears to be a harsh place where survival is paramount. Others experience life as a series of obligations and expectations. Some hold fast to an ideological worldview without subjecting it to the scrutiny of reality. The fundamental error within the realm of maya is the unwavering belief that our perception of the world is the sole truth, and our beliefs are absolute. Those who dare to diverge from this accepted truth can face resistance.

It's essential to remember that this is all a grand illusion! Certain illusions are necessary for our existence in the material world and for accumulating essential experiences. We must accept these illusions as our present reality at this stage of development. Yet, there are also unnecessary illusions that hinder our personal growth.

Exercise: Seeking a New Perspective

1. Stepping into the awareness of this illusion encourages us to reevaluate everything we've experienced, witnessed, and constructed, enabling us to see the world with fresh eyes. It encourages self-reflection and a series of questions: Do I truly desire this? Are my current surroundings and relationships aligned with my desires? Is my current path fulfilling? If the answer is no, it's time for change.
2. A willingness to see the world from a different perspective entails renaming things, forming new connections, taking new actions, exploring both ourselves and the world with renewed curiosity. Breaking free from preconceived notions can be achieved by either forgetting or conscious choice, and the power to decide lies within our hands. However, it is crucial to understand that consciously embracing the new doesn't erase the knowledge and experiences of the past; it enriches our being. This uniqueness defines our path and shapes distinctive relationships in our lives.
3. Where are you willing to view the world with fresh eyes? What attracts you? In which aspects of your life can you seek a new perspective? Where do you encounter duality in your life?

ART THAT EVOKES THE SQUARE

- *Cloud Atlas* (2012): This film directed by the Wachowskis weaves multiple narratives across different timelines, emphasizing the idea that individual actions and experiences are interconnected across time and space. It explores themes of reincarnation, karma, and the impact of choices.

- *Duality* by Rene Magritte: This surrealist painting (1937, oil on canvas, private collection) depicts a man with his back turned, revealing a faceless mirror image, symbolizing the concept of personal duality.
- *Life of Pi* by Yann Martel: Both the book and it's movie adaptation follow a young boy's efforts to survive while stranded on a lifeboat with a Bengal tiger. The narrative constantly questions our perception of reality, while simultaneously reflecting the core of human existence.

3 Krodha ANGER

When we are no longer able to change a situation, we are challenged to change ourselves.

VIKTOR FRANKL

In the midst of life's twists and turns, discord occasionally rears its head, culminating in that all-too-familiar feeling of anguish. But at its root, anger is not chaos. It is a signal. If the anger stems from the incongruence between our expectations and reality, we ask ourselves, "Why didn't it go as planned?" but the deeper question is: "Where did this rigid belief in my expectations come from?" Instead of pushing anger down, pause and listen. What needs to evolve or change? Because in its purest form, anger is not destruction—it is direction.

The duality of the mind tends to categorize everything in the world as right or wrong, good or bad. Yet, the world encompasses a diverse spectrum, and so does the individual. Both what is deemed good and what is disowned as bad reside within the player. The world acts as an expansive mirror, and when a person encounters something reflecting those suppressed "negative" traits, a storm of anger brews. The immediate reaction is, "This is unacceptable! It shouldn't be this way!" The urge to eliminate, alter, or obliterate it arises. It's worth noting that we typically experience anger toward those with whom we can relate. For instance, what might be tolerated in a stranger can be met with severe judgment when seen in a loved one. Conversely, something that elicits condescension and a smile from a foreigner may trigger anger when observed in a fellow countryman.

If someone claims not to experience anger, it is worth asking whether they are bottling up that anger, harboring it internally, or concealing it within their body. Are they also not condemning themselves for harboring this anger? Suppressed anger can manifest through bodily symptoms like gastritis, ulcers, injuries, or dental problems, often as unwelcome messages from the body.

Often, we find ourselves dealing with inward anger. Upon deep introspection, one may discover that anger toward another person is, at its core, anger toward oneself for failing to stand up in a conflict. A person gets angry because they realize that they have not taken what they could have or should have taken, or because they have not demanded what they could have or should have demanded. Instead of insisting on and taking what they lack, a person gets angry at those from whom they did not demand or take it. Such anger is a substitute for one's own actions and the result of not having realized them. It paralyzes us, makes us weak, and often possesses us for a very long time. Such anger can arise as a defense against one's own feelings of love—instead of expressing one's love, one gets angry at those whom one loves. Such anger arises in childhood when it is caused by an interrupted movement toward a loved one. Later, in similar situations, the childhood experience automatically repeats itself, gaining strength from that initial interruption.

A person may harbor anger toward someone because of an upsetting incident but may be unwilling to admit it. In such cases, this anger is used as a shield, deflecting the consequences of one's own guilt onto another. This form of anger serves as a means of evading responsibility for one's actions toward others, rendering the individual inert, paralyzed, and weakened.

Furthermore, some individuals carry and exhibit anger they have learned from or on behalf of others. For instance, when a member of a group suppresses their anger, it often manifests in another member of the same group, typically the one with the least apparent reason for anger. In family dynamics, this weaker member is often the child. For example, if a mother is upset with the father but chooses to bottle up her feelings, one of the children might outwardly express anger toward the father.

Conversely, the weakest member of a group not only becomes a vessel for the anger of others but also a target for their frustration. If a subordinate is upset with a superior but keeps it in check, they may frequently displace their anger onto a less powerful member of the organization.[1] Similarly, if a husband is angry with his wife but suppresses it, the child may end up suffering instead of the mother.

Individuals bearing this adopted anger may be consumed by rage, often maintaining a sense of pride and self-righteousness. Yet, their anger and its associated actions draw from external energy and the rights of others. Consequently, those carrying this anger remain weakened and their endeavors prove futile. The recipients of transferred anger might feel strong and justified in their suffering, as they recognize the injustice, but they too remain weakened, and their suffering serves no purpose.

But anger is not a purely negative emotion. So why does it exist in the great tapestry of human emotions? Is there anything good about it? Surprisingly, yes. It's a signal, a messenger from the Universe or a higher consciousness, announcing that our limits have been broken. A reminder that we can no longer tolerate what's unfolding. It is a stark revelation of our failure to set clear boundaries or articulate our expectations of the world and its inhabitants.

In this tangled web of emotions, anger holds a truth—a deeply personal truth. Embracing and harnessing this authenticity, even in the face of difficult choices, becomes an imperative. Within the flames of anger lies a wealth of unadulterated honesty, a beacon to guide us through the maze of existence.

Exercise: A Call for Transformation

1. When our essence resists and protests, it underscores a compelling need for change. The inner force that surges within us serves as a clarion call for transformation. In these moments, we ask,
   "Why am I experiencing anger?"
   "Is it mine, or is it inherited?"
   "Is it a manipulative anger to avoid seeing unpleasant things?"
   "Am I good at setting boundaries and protecting what is mine?"
   "Is this anger a transformative call?"
   "What can I change right now?"
2. Try to answer these questions as they empower us to take action.

ART THAT EVOKES THE SQUARE

- *Turning Red* (2022): This Pixar animated film explores themes of adolescence, emotions, and personal anger.
- *American Beauty* (1999): This film portrays the simmering anger and dissatisfaction within a suburban family, highlighting the impact of personal struggles on daily life.
- *The Bell Jar* by Sylvia Plath: The protagonist, Esther Greenwood, grapples with feelings of anger and frustration as she confronts societal expectations and personal identity issues.

4 Lobha
GREED

We buy things we don't need with money we don't have to impress people we don't like.

CHUCK PALAHNIUK

The fourth square we explore, Lobha, is often translated as "greed" or "desire." Here, we encounter our longings, inclinations, and impulses, which form the basis of an essential question: "What is it that truly drives me?" This question is a linchpin, steering the course of our lives. To answer it, we must embark on the profound journey of self-discovery, beginning with the inquiry, "Who am I?" The earlier we attain clarity on this matter, the more time we gain to live in harmony with our values, ambitions, and objectives.

Greed, an emotional state marked by a sense of lack or inadequacy, resides within this realm. It breeds various fears, including the dread of scarcity, the fear of deprivation, and the apprehension of giving without receiving in return. Here, contentment remains elusive, leaving us with a perpetual sense that something is missing from our existing possessions. Often, we are oblivious to the abundance we possess, extending beyond material wealth. It may also manifest as a reluctance to express love, share experiences and knowledge, offer support, or allocate time to those dear to us. At the heart of it all lies fear—the fear of insufficiency, the fear of rejection when offering, and the fear of receiving nothing in return.

This fear may occasionally expand to encompass a broader apprehension of the world. Stepping out of our comfort zones can be seen as risky, potentially leading to harm. Consequently, we may withhold our wisdom and authentic selves, driven by the fear of vulnerability. When one remains ensnared by the grip of greed, they persist in dwelling in the shadow of scarcity, accumulating relentlessly in an effort to safeguard against potential losses, compounding their fear.

Our upbringing and the environments we grew up in often imposed demanding expectations upon us, making it challenging to experience unconditional acceptance. Relentless criticism, humiliation, or a lack of recognition for our accomplishments can erode our self-esteem and foster feelings of inferiority. Many individuals with an *inferiority complex* frequently measure themselves against others they perceive as better equipped to handle life's challenges.

Now that our parents are no longer in the picture, this incessant internal critique and control persist. Our inner critic chips away at our confidence, ambitions, and the joy of simply being. Indecision, fear of responsibility, insecurity, dread of making mistakes, avoidance of communication, the weight of personal failure, and the inability to attain our goals are all direct manifestations of the inferiority complex. The opposite of this inferiority complex is what Adler termed the *superiority complex*.[2] When feeling inferior, individuals may throw themselves into their work, achieving remarkable success to prove their worth, both to themselves and others.

Yet, to establish their self-worth, they must unequivocally demonstrate that others are, by comparison, "nothing." This can lead to a relentless pursuit of being the "King of the Mountain," striving to reach the top, pushing others down, and reveling in the fleeting moment of personal greatness. To compensate for their inferiority complex, individuals often engage in battles with family, friends, colleagues, and even political opponents, always vying to come out on top, regardless of the cost or risks involved. However, this ruthless pursuit offers them little satisfaction. Periods of decline are perceived as tragic, and moments of triumph are unsettling, as they are viewed as short-lived and demand constant, exhausting control over every aspect of life.

Though it's possible to achieve the desired outcome and maintain a position of dominance, two crucial nuances must be acknowledged. First, it's not a personal victory but rather a triumph of the inferiority complex, which has overshadowed the true self. Secondly, it's unclear how to effectively utilize this victory, as it serves no genuine purpose and often strains personal relationships. Inner peace remains elusive, as the pursuit of triumph exacts a high cost.

Exercise: Finding Your Authentic Desire

1. Even within the realm of desire, there lies the potential for personal growth. By acknowledging your current state of longing and seeking what might be missing in your life, you can consider constructive actions to enhance your well-being.
2. Perhaps you can develop new skills, establish a daily exercise routine, learn a foreign language, or engage in activities that resonate with you instead of merely fulfilling commitments you make to yourself. It's worth noting that we often find ourselves frustrated when others fail to keep promises they've made to us, yet we frequently struggle with honoring promises to ourselves, such as waking up earlier. How can we expect self-respect and self-trust if we consistently betray ourselves? Make a list of ten things that you can improve, and they will make you feel better.
3. Once you feel ready, create a list of ten desires or dreams, and then delve into a process of inquiry to discern their origins. It's essential to understand whether these aspirations are genuinely your own or if they've been influenced by societal or family pressures. For instance, when considering a career, it's valuable to question the source of your ambition. Is it an authentic desire, or does it primarily stem from a wish to fulfill a parental expectation or prove something to a family member? Unraveling the roots of these desires represents a pivotal step in the journey of self-discovery.

ART THAT EVOKES THE SQUARE

- *Table of the Seven Deadly Sins* by Hieronymus Bosch: Bosch's painting depicts greed as one of the seven deadly sins. It illustrates the destructive nature of greed and its consequences (c.1505–1510, oil on wood, Museo del Prado, Madrid).[3]

- *The Catcher in the Rye* by J. D. Salinger: The protagonist, Holden Caulfield, is a classic example of a character struggling with an inferiority complex as he navigates the challenges of adolescence.

5
Bhu Loka
PHYSICAL PLANE

We sing best in the branches of our genealogical tree.

René Char

The fifth square delves into the foundation, which represents all that is solid and physical within an individual. This square encompasses your body and your lineage, prompting you to inquire, "What is my relationship with my body? Can I truly empathize with my body's signals, including pain? Where in my body does pain accumulate, and what are the underlying reasons?" Many individuals grapple with inner demons such as fear, resentment, shame, distrust, aggression, and self-hatred, which manifest physically through muscle tension, aches, spasms, migraines, nervous tics, and other distinctive signs. Stress appears to become stored in our bodies, occasionally transforming life into a nightmare. It often leads to issues like insomnia, difficulties in interactions, challenges in sexual relationships, and trouble communicating with our own children. The degree of physical suffering is closely linked to the extent of inner suffering resulting from neglecting our own needs. Illness, in essence, becomes a physical expression of emotional and mental blockages. The purpose of illness is to capture the attention of individuals who may be unaware of or unwilling to acknowledge their unhealthy thoughts and emotions.

Bodily reactions may surface even when individuals are not direct subjects of traumatic experiences.[4] Simply witnessing a shocking event and identifying with it can trigger these reactions. For instance, observing violence, such as a child witnessing their mother being abused, can activate mirror neurons* in the brain, causing the person to experience the event as if it were happening to them. This overwhelming experience is fragmented into discrete elements, leading to the persistence of emotions, sounds, images, thoughts, and physical sensations linked to the trauma.

In the absence of deviations in the relationship with one's body, the focus shifts to examining one's lineage. The concept of Bhu Loka encompasses the land, the roots, and the connections with ancestors and descendants. Each lineage has its unique strengths and weaknesses that shape an individual's personality. This square encourages self-analysis of one's choice of lineage, what has been inherited from it, and the family configurations and programs that may limit or hinder personal growth.

An examination of relational structures from the perspective of family systems theory can reveal the presence of the law of hierarchy between the relatives. According to this law, each family member occupies a specific position of power based on their arrival to the group. Parents hold higher status than children, and older siblings take precedence over younger ones. However, this hierarchy is often violated. For example, children may show arrogance toward their parents, believing that they would be better off with other, more understanding and supportive caregivers. Such an attitude can extend to treating parents with contempt, especially if they are struggling with issues such as alcoholism, neglect, or abuse. The consequences of this arrogance can be harmful because it disrupts the flow of energy within the family, isolating the individual and forcing them into self-sufficiency. People who adopt this attitude may transfer their contempt for their parents to the world

*Mirror neurons in our brains play a pivotal role in experiencing empathy. They enable us to learn by replicating the actions of others and sharing their emotions, which is crucial for a sense of belonging and, ultimately, biological survival. These neurons strive to capture and deeply imprint information about the external world in our memories.

around them, resulting in dissatisfaction, a lack of self-esteem, and difficulty in forming healthy relationships and families.

People also sometimes may assume the role of caregiver for their parents, often due to chronic illness or temporary helplessness. This commitment to caregiving may come at the expense of their careers, personal lives, and even their own children, as they devote most of their energy to supporting their parents. The consequences of such choices can be profound, leading to unfulfilled personal lives and prolonged dependency on caregiving.

Cultivating a deep sense of gratitude toward one's parents is crucial to breaking free from such situations. Sincere gratitude allows individuals to accept the energy and support their parents provide, freeing them to live their lives independently. Expressing gratitude by acknowledging one's parents as the source of life enables individuals to mature and become whole persons.

Exercise: Acknowledging Your Body and Your Lineage

1. Begin your exploration by analyzing your physical pain and considering questions such as "What is my relationship with my body? Can I empathize with my body's signals, including pain? Where in my body is pain accumulating, and what are the causes?" The book *Your Body's Telling You: Love Yourself!* by Lise Bourbeau, a Canadian therapist, is a valuable resource that delves into the metaphysical causes of illness and disease, shedding light on the connection between our mental and emotional attitudes and physical ailments.
2. If you notice a breakdown in the hierarchy within your family system, take the opportunity to write two heartfelt letters—one to your mother and one to your father—expressing gratitude for giving you life. Acknowledge the rightful order in which they stand as older figures, and allow yourself to receive their energy and support, breaking free from isolation and self-sufficiency.
3. Make two lists: one of five characteristics of your family that limit you in your daily life, and another of five family traditions or patterns of behavior that support and empower you.

ART THAT EVOKES THE SQUARE

- *The Key in the Hand* by Chiharu Shiota: This artist's installations often explore themes of memory, identity, and the human body through intricate weblike structures that represent connections and entanglements. *The Key in the Hand* embodies personal history and emotional ties (2015, art installation with keys and yarn, Venice Art Biennale).
- *The Doctor* (1991): This film, starring William Hurt, follows the transformation of a doctor who becomes a patient and learns about the metaphysical aspects of illness, including the emotional and mental factors that contribute to disease.
- *The Royal Tenenbaums* (2001): Wes Anderson's film delves into the complexities of a dysfunctional family's hierarchy and how it impacts family members' lives and interactions.

6 Moha ATTACHMENTS

He who has a why to live can bear almost any how.

FRIEDRICH NIETZSCHE

The sixth square, called Moha or Attachments, represents a square that all players inevitably encounter during the course of the game. The initial roll of the dice leads all players to this very square. It's a state in which we accept the rules of the game, the conditions of *maya* (the illusion of the material world), and the social norms of our place of birth, and the values held by those around us. Moha grants the soul the right to reincarnate and live again. But the question arises—are we learning and growing, or still stumbling through the same patterns?

Our beliefs often serve as boundaries that restrict our actions, often rooted in a fear of venturing beyond those boundaries. We ensnare ourselves in these beliefs to create an illusion of order and security. Statements such as "I need coffee to stay alert; I can't function without it," "I can't survive without that person," or "I can only earn a sufficient income if . . ." embody the basis of all human addictions. While addictions such as alcohol, drugs, and gambling are socially condemned, you may discover that a tumultuous love affair or obsessive devotion to someone is simply another form of dependence on another individual. When our internal state is dependent on something or someone external, we are dealing with an addiction. Life makes no distinction between alcohol addiction and love addiction; the underlying pattern is the same.

The challenge arises when individuals perceive themselves as separate from the rest of the world, dividing it into the familiar and the unknown, the understandable and the hostile. Such individuals strive to establish themselves firmly in their own world, resulting in rigid perspectives and the belief that their views are the only correct ones. They tend to surround themselves with like-minded individuals and possessions, and structure their lives according to their established preferences. This leaves little room for new experiences or alternative viewpoints.

It is imperative to recognize that illusions about the world and dependencies on people, possessions, and habits not only cloud one's perception of the world but also obscure one's sense of self. Amid these attachments, individuals struggle to decipher their true desires and needs. They persist in their habitual behaviors and interpret situations as they always have. Changing one's worldview can be profoundly challenging while trapped in this square. However, once a person is in the game, they are ready for transformation. The Moha square encourages questioning of fundamentals, including deeply held beliefs that may seem unshakable.

Exercise: Finding Opposing Viewpoints

1. Make a list of ten perspectives on the world and life.
2. For each perspective, write down the opposing viewpoint. For exam-

ple, if the perspective you wrote down is "Life is unfair," then the opposing viewpoint is "Life is just."

3. State three supporting arguments for each opposing viewpoint.

ART THAT EVOKES THE SQUARE

- *I'm Thinking of Ending Things* (2020): Directed by Charlie Kaufman, this psychological drama follows a young woman who joins her boyfriend on a road trip to visit his parents' remote farm. As the journey unfolds, the woman's thoughts take a surreal turn, and the boundaries between reality and imagination blur. The film delves into themes of identity, loneliness, and the passage of time.

7 Mada VANITY

Everyone can be proud, even of not having pride.

POLINA RUD

Mada translates from Sanskrit as "vanity." But what does *vanity* truly mean? It's the realm of our self-deceptions, the illusions we harbor about ourselves. If the previous stage, the sixth square, challenged the rules we've accepted, here we delve into the beliefs we hold about ourselves. Consider statements like "I mustn't make mistakes," "People will judge me if I . . . ," "I don't have enough talent," "I don't have enough experience," "I am too old or young for this," "I am better than others," "I will do everything by myself," and so on and on.

Our innate desire to stand out and be exceptional is a fundamental aspect of human nature. This aspiration has been deeply woven into the fabric of our being, whether it takes the form of wanting to be faster, taller, stronger, or—paradoxically—weaker than others. While the notion of seeking weakness may appear surprising, it reflects an alternative means of seeking recognition for those who may struggle to distinguish themselves in more traditional ways. This somewhat unconventional desire to be considered "weaker" can manifest as a kind of competitive vulnerability, a subtle game of one-upmanship where individuals vie for sympathy and attention. It often becomes particularly evident within family dynamics, notably in mother-child relationships. As children grow into adulthood, asserting their independence and shedding the need for obedience, a power shift occurs. The matriarch, who once held unquestioned authority, may find this transition challenging and may respond by adopting a victim role, invoking sympathy and attention. Is this, too, a manifestation of vanity? Undoubtedly. It is another facet of vanity, epitomized by the belief, "I am the weakest," demanding a spotlight.

In many instances, people have valid reasons for feeling vain, whether those reasons are real or imagined. The important point is that vanity creates a division between a person and others. The illusion of being slightly better or superior to others widens the gap, leaving a person isolated and yearning to prove their worth.

When we strive to become the best version of ourselves, we inadvertently fragment our identity by concealing the parts we disapprove of. Society teaches us to be good but often neglects to instruct us on accepting the so-called bad within us. We've been conditioned to believe that our darker aspects must be hidden, contained, and controlled, lest others uncover our true selves. Vanity, in this context, serves as a mask for a lack of self-love. Denying what we consider unworthy usually leads to low self-esteem. Vanity then appears on the other end of the spectrum, serving as a counterbalance. Here, one becomes dependent on the opinions of others: Why bother if it won't gain their approval? Why create something beautiful, a piece of art or a song, if it won't be purchased? And if what we create fails to satisfy ourselves but triggers the desire for others to covet it, that's acceptable. When what we create is validated by others, we feel like we've reached the pinnacle.

The primary fallacy in the Vanity square is the tendency to equate one's worth with the outcomes of their endeavors and the opinions of others about them. In this square, the player cannot see themselves clearly, nor do they want to acknowledge their entirety. They only know how to love themselves through the accolades of others. In this space, a person confuses authenticity with being "better." They perceive their individuality by comparing themselves to others and comparing others to themselves without recognizing their uniqueness. Friedrich Nietzsche defined *vanity* as "the fear of appearing original: it is, therefore, a lack of pride, but not necessarily a lack of originality."[5] Sometimes, even objectively "great" individuals find themselves trapped in this square, finding it challenging to understand why the vanity that drives them to excel is a mistake. However, ponder this: Atop that pedestal, there is room for just one. It is a lonely and desolate place. To step out of this square, one must relinquish the belief that personal achievements make them superior to others. Each person is distinct and incomparable. We must strive to bridge the divide with others and channel our energy into discovering our authenticity.

It's crucial to comprehend that vanity is a natural facet of the ego. As long as we partake in the human experience, vanity will remain a constant companion. There's no need to eradicate this quality. Rather, acknowledge it with humor and continually question your self-perceptions.

Exercise: Reset Your Beliefs About Yourself

1. The square invites you to reset everything you know about yourself. Before rolling the die, contemplate your beliefs. Ask yourself questions such as the following:
   "Who am I?"
   "What roles am I playing right now?"
   "What do I believe in?"
   "What do I excel at?"
   "What do I possess?"

2. Write down three justifications for an opposite belief. For example, if your original belief is "I don't have enough talent to start my own business," one justification for its opposite could be "I *do* have enough talent to start my own business, because I excel at problem-solving and collaboration."
3. Make a list of ten points and come up with opposing justifications for those beliefs. Be honest and authentic.

ART THAT EVOKES THE SQUARE

- *The Devil's Dictionary* by Ambrose Bierce: Bierce's satirical definitions often poke fun at human vanity and pretentiousness.
- *American Psycho* (2000): This film, based on the novel by Bret Easton Ellis, follows the life of a narcissistic investment banker who becomes a serial killer, highlighting the toxic effects of vanity.

8 Matsara AVIDITY

Avidity is essentially the fear-driven hunger for more.

POLINA RUD

The eighth square, known as Matsara, differs significantly from square 4, Greed. While Greed revolves around the individual's sense of lack, Matsara is translated as "avidity" or "dissatisfaction," the individual's reluctance to share what they have. It is important to note that this is not limited to material possessions. To better understand the psychological mechanisms at play, let's explore examples related to material wealth, but keep in mind that the same principles can apply to emotions, knowledge, information, time, or attention.

Why do people tend to hoard resources? There may be several reasons. It often stems from past experiences in which a person faced scarcity or lacked something essential, creating a lingering fear that their resources might suddenly disappear. For example, if a person previously lacked money and associated it with stability and security, even if they acquire wealth, they may still perceive losing money as a threat to their security. Consequently, sharing or lending money to others becomes a perceived threat to their stability.

Another facet of greed is the fear of overpaying or paying even a slightly higher price than the average. For example, someone might avoid a salon that charges $105 for a haircut (when the average price is $100) because they believe they are being cheated. This behavior is often rooted in a strong belief that everyone is out to cheat them, which in turn may be a projection of their willingness to cheat others for personal gain. This mistrust is related to their self-worth or self-esteem, where they believe, "I am only important because I have money, and everyone wants to take advantage of me." In this case, money replaces self-esteem in their worldview.

Money is also used to gain importance, power, and superiority. Some people buy the loyalty of others or clear a path for themselves. Money and the power it confers can be seen as an attempt to fulfill infantile fantasies of omnipotence. Among those who seek power through money, there are different types.[6] Manipulators, for example, use money to exploit the vanity and greed of others, which makes them feel less helpless and frustrated. They may not feel guilty about exploiting others, but gradually their energy dwindles as they constantly humiliate and neglect others, leading to eventual disappointment.

The Empire Builder type often displays tremendous independence and self-confidence, suppressing or denying their dependency on others while trying to make others dependent on them. Many end up lonely and isolated, especially in old age. The Godfather type uses money for bribery and control, masking their need for public respect with anger and hypersensitivity to humiliation. They attract the weak and defenseless, suppressing initiative and independence while surrounding themselves with second-rate sycophants.

Money is a common means for acquiring love, loyalty, and self-respect. The principle of reciprocity is crucial in gift-giving, leading many to believe that reciprocal gifts indicate love and care. Some people try to buy love and respect by visiting prostitutes, making charitable contributions, or spoiling children. Their actions are driven by a fear of feeling unloved and a desire to avoid rejection and worthlessness by pleasing others with their generosity. However, they may find it difficult to receive reciprocal love, and their generosity may mask genuine hostility toward those on whom they depend. Conversely, some individuals literally sell love, affection, and flattery to boost their egos. They find it easy to imitate this behavior and naturally attract those who want to buy love.

Dissatisfaction is another facet of avidity. In the Matsara space, individuals struggle with an unrelenting sense that something is missing, a pervasive dissatisfaction with their current circumstances. Dissatisfied people tend to remain dissatisfied with their lives, regardless of their accomplishments or possessions. They constantly yearn for more, which has a significant impact on how they approach money and the need to acquire it. Such individuals often experience inner dissatisfaction, discomfort, and a general dissatisfaction with life. Paradoxically, the more they try to change their circumstances, the more intense their feelings of inadequacy become. I once had a personal session with a young woman who sought to address various issues, one of which was her strong desire to travel. Interestingly, even when she found herself in foreign countries, her persistent dissatisfaction remained. Such states of dissatisfaction cannot be resolved by external changes alone.

In such situations, here is another important question to consider: If I were to tell you that your life would remain exactly as it is now for the rest of your days, would you be content? If your response is that everything must change, it indicates that the lesson hasn't been fully grasped. In these cases, it's vital to genuinely embrace your present circumstances, whether that means residing in a small apartment, dealing with limited resources, facing challenges related to starting a family, or experiencing unemployment. Discovering the broader purpose behind these situations and recognizing their potential secondary benefits is crucial. This concept of secondary benefits is explored further in the chapter "Basic Archetypes," p. 31.

If you're always resisting and feeling dissatisfied with your current situation, you might end up expending all your energy in an ongoing struggle. This doesn't imply that nothing should ever change, but it's essential to realize that at various points in our lives, we have the opportunities and resources needed to progress along our individual paths. Don't hesitate to share with others, and when you give, whether it's emotions, time, experience, money, or attention, avoid expecting anything in return. Steer clear of falling into the mindset of, "I gave my all, what did I get in return?" Such thoughts can lead to manipulative behavior. True giving doesn't mean self-sacrifice; it involves giving from a place of abundance, where your own needs are fulfilled. When there's no sense of greed, sharing happens naturally from the overflow of your resources, with the knowledge that you'll have more to share in the future.

Exercise: Sharing What You Have

1. Take a moment to write down what you can share with people in the next twenty-four hours. It could be an emotion or a piece of knowledge or skill.
2. Often people accumulate extensive knowledge and skills but fail to share them. It's important to explore the reasons for this resistance—is it a fear judgment, a sense of inadequacy, or a fear of not having enough?
3. Think about what you can share right now, and use the secondary benefit concepts described on p. 32–33 to understand why you haven't done so before and what might be underlying this reluctance.
4. Once you've explored your resistance, gather your courage and share what you have.

ART THAT EVOKES THE SQUARE

- *There Will Be Blood* (2007): Directed by Paul Thomas Anderson, this film tells the story of a ruthless oilman driven by greed and dissatisfaction.

9
Kama Loka
DESIRES

The only way out is through.

Robert Frost

To be human is to feel. It's our most fragile gift—and our most divine. This square encompasses pain, pleasure, orgasms, and all the sensations we encounter through our physical bodies. Yet we often treat this gift with suspicion and numb, suppress, or sedate it. But pain is not the opposite of life, but the thread that gives texture to joy, depth to love, and meaning to growth. It is through the body that the soul learns.

It is crucial to remain attuned to our feelings, to honor our sensations, and to trust our innate instincts. Sometimes, an individual endures an intensely painful sensory encounter and subsequently seeks to evade it by any means possible. More often than not, the response is self-isolation and a solemn vow to never again open themselves up to sensory experiences. This self-imposed exile extends beyond merely avoiding pain; it also involves relinquishing the capacity to experience other emotions, such as happiness or love. While there may not be a switch in our bodies to selectively erase a particular memory or traumatic episode, there exists a metaphorical circuit breaker that can promptly extinguish all emotions and the ability to feel altogether.

Our sojourn in this life is intrinsically tied to sensory experience. Finding ourselves within this square prompts us to acknowledge the sensory dimension of existence, to pose questions like "What am I feeling in this moment?" "What do my emotions signify, and what messages do they convey?" and "Am I allowing myself to authentically express what I feel?"

Emotions are, in essence, "energy in motion." Suppressing this energy begets obstructions. For instance, when a person feels anger but societal norms deem it inappropriate to display that emotion, or if their family has forbidden its expression, they may repress it. This emotional stifling results in energetic blockages that can have adverse effects on health and overall quality of life down the road.

Conversely, an individual can become overly immersed in their emotions. Rather than harness their desires as catalysts for personal growth, they risk becoming ensnared in their passions and daydreams. They lament to friends and loved ones, exclaiming, "Oh, the suffering I endure!" or "How I yearn for a different life!" However, their actions do not align with their words, leading to an exhausting cycle of emotional turmoil that offers no real change or progress.

Yet another pitfall on the sensory level is the inability to recognize the overwhelming feelings coursing through one's being. A person may sense that something is amiss, yet they grapple with deciphering the nature of their emotions. Your psyche might have repressed emotions as a response to a traumatic experience, with the intention of burying those feelings to prevent a recurrence; this is the most common cause. However, at times, repressed emotions could be linked to a karmic experience. For instance, during a truth-validation session, one of my clients and I uncovered that in one of his past lives, he impulsively took another person's life. Consequently, in his current life, it may seem unsafe for him to openly express his emotions lest they get out of control and cause harm. Another client of mine, in one of her past incarnations, existed within a sociopolitical milieu where marriages were solely based on deliberate and strategic choices. To endure an unloving spouse throughout her lifetime, she had to turn off her heart and her capacity to feel anything at all.

If you realize that your emotions have been blocked for an extended period, be prepared to experience emotions you've suppressed in the past as soon as you allow yourself to feel. Emotions don't come with expiration dates. You might find yourself responding emotionally to everyday situations, and that's perfectly normal—there's no need to chastise yourself for it. If a heartwarming cartoon moves you to tears, let them flow. If you feel like getting angry, allow yourself to be angry. Eventually, the pendulum will settle into a neutral position.

Exercise: Initiate the Process of Unblocking Your Emotions

1. As a daily practice, spend some time in a dark room while gazing at the flame of a candle. This activity aids in relaxation and also cleanses the eyes, as the flame can stimulate tears. After a few days or weeks, you may find yourself able to cry—this is your body's initial signal that it's acceptable to start feeling again.
2. After a week of this practice, take a minute to sit down and recite the following affirmations:
   "I acknowledge and embrace that I locked away my feelings for self-preservation. I am now reclaiming my ability to feel and be vulnerable. I can be vulnerable in this world while maintaining healthy boundaries. I am unblocking my emotions."
3. Don't be apprehensive; as a bonus from these practices, your intuition will also unlock, allowing your inner voice to guide you back onto the right path. Blocked emotions often coincide with blocked intuition, leading to uncertainty about what to do, how to do it, and where to go.
4. If you realize that your emotions aren't blocked, jot down three situations when your intuition guided you to make the correct decisions or saved your life. Revisit those moments when you felt as though you were being spoken to, guided by an inner prompting. Try to recapture that state.

5. If you recognize that your life is predominantly governed by one or more emotions, list them out and contemplate how you can express these emotions in a balanced and harmonious manner.

ART THAT EVOKES THE SQUARE

- *Donnie Darko* (2001): The main character grapples with repressed emotions and a sense of impending doom, which drives the narrative.

LEVEL 2
ENGAGING WITH OTHERS

On the second row, the player begins to break free from their shell. Now, there are other people in their life besides their family and themselves, and they have to learn to interact with them. Here, a person strives to find that balance in communication where they are open to others, ready to engage in a dialogue, and willing to listen to the other person, but at the same time, they know their limits. They don't sacrifice their interests for the benefit of someone else, nor do they put themselves in a dependent position on others.

On this level, individuals consciously start engaging with the world. The more the player opens up to the world, the more the world reflects their emotional states—in people's behavior, attitudes, and the situations they encounter. The world presents challenges and opportunities, and it's a mirror for the player's strengths and weaknesses. Thus, the world addresses you and anticipates your reaction. What emotions will you experience from the events that unfold? How will you behave?

The second row invites you to pay attention to aspects of life related to friendships, work, love, and intimate relationships. Do you have expectations from the world and other people, placing hopes on them? Are you possessive or do you allow your loved ones their freedom? Are you open to learning from others, or are you consumed by jealousy? Are you judgmental or compassionate?

10

Shuddhi

PURIFICATION

The mind is like a parachute. It doesn't work unless it's open.

FRANK ZAPPA

You've reached the second level of the game. At this point, you have already become acquainted with yourself, your desires, your extremes, and your emotions. The first step toward leading a conscious life is purification. Here, it becomes evident that not everything in your environment, not all that people aspire to, is suitable for you. In this square, you learn to distinguish the external from the self. How can you achieve this? How can you rid yourself of social and interpersonal influences?

1. Assess your surroundings, which means removing toxic people from your life.
2. Reconsider your diet: Remove products that burden your body, making it feel sluggish. This can hinder your intuition and your ability to make sound decisions. Learn the basic principles of ayurveda, and identify the dominant *dosha* in your body to harmonize your diet.
3. Manage the sources (social networks, television, online resources, email newsletters) through which information enters your mind. What kind of information is it? How relevant is it to you? Conversely, does it divert your attention from genuinely important matters, promoting procrastination?

From time to time, it is vital to partake in purification practices, such as abstaining from salt for a month, dancing with your eyes closed, or engaging in Vipassana meditation, where you and those around you maintain silence for at least fourteen days. Sensory deprivation enables us to purify our perception, ultimately enhancing our hearing or vision. After purification, you free yourself from all that is unnecessary, and the arrow propels you swiftly to the third level.

Exercise: Purification Practice

1. Select a purification method that resonates with you and seems suitable for your current state. Choose from any of those mentioned in this book, or from any other source that speaks to you. Begin this practice after completing the game.
2. Listen to a healing 432 Hz meditation (search online for "432 Hz binaural beats").

ART THAT EVOKES THE SQUARE

We're striving to cleanse ourselves of any influences that could shape our perception. Therefore, I won't disturb you with any artistic examples.

This is the first arrow of the game, the arrow of purification! As we cleanse our senses, we enhance our capacity to delicately perceive the world, empowering us to decode valuable insights, and steadily advancing us toward the square of Heaven (23).

11
Gandharva
ENTERTAINMENT

What we fear doing most is usually what we most need to do.

Tim Ferriss

Entertainment is the unique expression of your soul that sets you apart from others, where your soul qualities shine through. It's a process where the outcome doesn't matter; you are fully immersed in the moment, enjoying the experience. Entertainment revitalizes us, giving us strength and energy. So, this square invites you to consider these questions:

If you were free of work and responsibilities, what would you choose to do?

Now that you have the opportunity, what calls to you?

In the midst of your daily responsibilities, it's important to make time for activities that bring you joy, that showcase your individuality, and that ignite your passion. Do you allow yourself to have fun, or do you see it as a waste of time?

The challenge is to choose the right form of entertainment. If you feel drained and unenthusiastic about returning to your duties after indulging in entertainment, it may not have been the right fit. This could also be a sign of an addiction to positive emotions, where entertainment becomes an escape from responsibility. For example, returning from a vacation full of energy and renewed enthusiasm for work is beneficial entertainment. Conversely, coming back feeling discouraged, helpless, and unmotivated suggests that your short-term escape strategy isn't effective.

In a state of positive-emotional addiction, a person doesn't deal with life's lessons; instead, they seek a new emotional fix that intensifies over time. This pattern can lead to various addictions, whether it's alcoholism, gambling, or socially accepted addictions such as the pursuit of new experiences or places. Take extreme sports, for example, where the adrenaline rush and intense emotions become addictive. People seek these heightened sensations because they're missing in their everyday lives or because they want to achieve a thought-free state. During activities such as skydiving, the mind remains clear, focused solely on survival, unencumbered by other concerns. The pursuit of such activities may stem from a desire to replicate the clear mental state that is elusive in everyday life. This type of entertainment is considered escapism and does not produce positive results in the long run.

Exercise: Choose Your Activity and Take Action

Imagine a scenario where work and responsibilities are no longer a concern. What activity would you pick? If singing comes to mind, take that phone and call—right now—any singing tutor or music school that you'll find on the internet to arrange your very first lesson. Take action, don't delay.

ART THAT EVOKES THE SQUARE

- *Dead Poets Society* (1989): Directed by Peter Weir, this film explores the transformative power of poetry and literature as a form of entertainment and inspiration. It highlights how these pursuits can help individuals break free from societal constraints and express themselves.

12 Irasya ENVY

Comparison is the thief of joy.

THEODORE ROOSEVELT

Irasya, a Sanskrit term, means "envy." But what is envy? It's the act of comparing yourself to others. When you do this, you leave no room for your own unique path and see yourself as someone else, ideally positioned in perfect circumstances. Comparison leads to competition and the desire to prove your superiority, whether to others or even to yourself. But why go down that road? It's far more beneficial to step out of the race and embrace your individuality. No one can be better than you because you are unique.

So why does this urge to compare arise? It comes from insecurity and a lack of understanding of your own uniqueness. You may not have had a role model to confirm the normality of your personality and reassure you that all is well. When the psyche lacks such reassurance, the incessant search for validation begins: "Tell me I'm normal, worthy, and capable."

Envy arises because of the perceived societal approval given to those who achieve professional success, own a home, own a car, have a family, or meet other conventional standards of a "good" person. Society has a predetermined idea of what's decent and right, an average ideal to which people are expected to aspire. If you don't conform, you may feel that there is something wrong with you, and that's when envy rears its ugly head.

But why does envy exist if it's such a negative emotion? Envy can be a mirror that reflects your untapped potential. It's important to pay attention to your inner reactions. When you feel envy, explore what triggers the emotion and toward whom. Perhaps you can cultivate qualities in yourself that are present in others.

Envy isn't just about comparison. On a deeper subconscious level, it's the belief that happiness will come when certain events occur, such as when your children grow up, when you achieve financial prosperity, when you take a break, or when you achieve enlightenment. Everyone has their own unique "when" that marks their vision of a better future. Instead of waiting for these events, it's important to appreciate and find joy in the present. If you are struggling to experience happiness, consider changing your environment—your interactions, activities, or daily routine.

How envy can manifest, either from you or directed at you:

- Downplaying the accomplishments of others, attributing their success to luck rather than hard work.
- Giving insincere compliments or passive-aggressive praise to those who have achieved success.
- Imitating another person's speech or style in order to become no worse, and often better, than they are.
- Complaining about the unfairness of how some people seem to have it easy while others work tirelessly.
- Envy may show up in the way people talk about mutual acquaintances or celebrities, often sneaking into their conversations.

Exercise: Analyze Your Envy

1. Reflect on three situations in which you've found yourself comparing yourself to another person. Envy is an emotion that many people tend to deny, often due to its negative connotations in society. Nevertheless, most of us have experienced it in some form or another. Analyze how it surfaces in your life.
2. Identify and jot down five distinctive personality traits that set you apart from others.

ART THAT EVOKES THE SQUARE

- *Metamorphoses* by Ovid: In this literary masterpiece, the theme of envy is prevalent in the story of Daedalus and his talented apprentice Talos. Daedalus, a skilled craftsman, becomes consumed by envy as he observes Talos's remarkable abilities, leading to a tragic turn of events. This classical work by Ovid provides an early exploration of the destructive nature of envy, illustrating its impact on human actions and relationships.

The primary purpose of this snake is to teach you to enjoy the journey of life itself, emphasizing that life is about experiencing existence. When you are guided by Irasya (Envy, square 12) you descend the tail of the snake to encounter Matsara (Avidity, square 8), also known as "dissatisfaction."

13
Antariksha
NULLITY

You are never too old to set another goal or to dream a new dream.

C. S. Lewis

The state of square 13, Nullity, may not be the most pleasant, but it is of great importance. Life is a series of ups and downs. At times we exude energy, brimming with ideas and enthusiasm, while at other times we may feel helpless, unworthy, and lost in a fog of uncertainty. In these moments, our usual methods and tools seem ineffective, even though they may have served us well in the past.

It's similar to the experience of a first-grader embarking on their educational journey. They are, at the beginning, aware of the challenges ahead, but unsure of how to overcome them. To enter this state, one must once again assume the role of a student and seek guidance from those who have walked a similar path.

This state also reminds us not to fear becoming a student again. Your past accomplishments and skills remain intact, only now they are enriched with new knowledge appropriate to this stage of life. Rebooting as a student means recognizing that great achievements take time and patience. The anticipation of a new beginning can be intriguing, prompting questions such as "How will I walk this path?" and "Who will I become along the way?" If you feel anxiety, it may be because you are too focused on the distant endpoint. Return to the present and focus on the first step.

Exercise: Advice for Your Journey

1. Seek out those who can guide you to point B, analyze their experiences, and ask for their advice when needed.
2. Consider what small action you can take right now on this unknown journey.

ART THAT EVOKES THE SQUARE

- *Composition VIII* by Wassily Kandinsky: This painting embodies a vision of a new world being born from the ruins of the old, reflecting a global desire for reconstruction, peace, and progress after World War I. The geometric shapes evoke a sense of emerging order from chaos, breaking away from outdated systems and embracing the promise of modernity and human ingenuity, as symbolized by the depiction of the compass (1923, oil on canvas, Guggenheim Museum, New York).
- "The Road Not Taken" by Robert Frost: This poem illustrates the idea of choosing a new path in life. The speaker reflects on a pivotal moment where they chose the less-traveled path, signifying a new direction and exploration.

14
Bhuvar Loka
ASTRAL PLANE

Most people do not listen with the intent to understand; they listen with the intent to reply.

Stephen R. Covey

Bhuvar Loka is the subtle bridge between Earth and Sky—where body meets soul and sexuality awakens as consciousness. However, it encompasses more than just sexual relations; it's about the *connections* we form with others. It's where we start to learn the intricate craft of interaction, cultivating empathy and mutual understanding. These skills are pivotal for success in any endeavor because we are inherently social beings. To interact authentically is to listen—not dominate—in order to protect your own truth without manipulating or suppressing another. The crucial lesson is to listen both to yourself and to others and to recognize that everything unfolding around you serves your growth and development.

Exercise: Explore Your Interpersonal Patterns

1. Go back and review the interpretations of the archetypes the Lovers and the Hanged Man from the chapter "Basic Archetypes."
2. Can you see any similarities between the negative aspects of these archetypes and your behavioral and psychological patterns?
3. What are your current relationship concerns, whether they pertain to sexual relationships, communication, or friendships?

ART THAT EVOKES THE SQUARE

- *Silver Linings Playbook* (2012): Directed by David O. Russell, this film depicts the complex dynamics between the two protagonists,

Pat and Tiffany. They both struggle with mental health issues and develop a codependent relationship. Their quest for acceptance and stability forms the central theme of the story.

- *Who's Afraid of Virginia Woolf?* by Edward Albee: This play delves into the manipulative, dysfunctional marriage of George and Martha. Their dependence on each other, coupled with a constant power struggle, leads to intense conflict and emotional turmoil.

15 Naga Loka
FANTASY

> *Dreams are illustrations . . . from the book your soul is writing about you.*
>
> Marsha Norman

Fantasies can have both positive and negative implications. On the one hand, every fantasy serves as a beacon to the vast array of possibilities we could potentially achieve. Anything that comes to mind already exists within the realm of possibility and thus offers the potential for realization. Dreams and fantasies serve as a means by which the soul communicates our capabilities and preserves its impulses and desires. Understanding the meaning of your dreams is tantamount to heeding your soul's guidance, which allows you to align your life with your true desires. The central goal is to construct a life that reflects your true desires.

In this personal mental space, individuals revel in their freedom to pursue any inclination or experience that piques their interest. This flexibility serves as a valuable resource, allowing individuals to explore their dreams and recognize their authenticity. By imagining their desires within the domain of fantasy, individuals can assess whether these desires are truly in line with their own, whether they can make these dreams a reality.

On the other hand, there is a less favorable aspect to this state. Fantasies often function as an escape from reality, manifesting as unfounded reveries that distract individuals from their tangible goals. These idle dreams give rise to an illusory hope that can later turn into sorrow: "My dreams never came true; I'm unsure of the direction my life is taking, and I've always wished for something different."

What's more, fantasies are not always pleasant. Often, individuals create subconscious images, sometimes tinged with fear and anxiety, as they grapple with uncertainty. These scenarios represent a distinct human game: conjuring up and then fearing, worrying, and suffering. Caught in the web of their fantasies, individuals begin to blur the boundaries between reality and imagination. They find themselves dwelling in imaginary relationships, oblivious to real connections with those around them. Personal fantasies can also interfere with self-awareness, making it difficult for individuals to understand themselves and adjust their behavior for effective interactions in society.

Individuals may also seek refuge in fantasies through means such as alcohol, drugs, video games, or trance practices/experiences that promote sensory immersion. However, these escapades interfere with the acquisition of genuine experiences, and living within these illusions ultimately drains the individual. This underscores the importance of mastering the control of one's fantasies. By learning to navigate the transition between reality and fantasy, individuals gain the ability to realize their dreams in the real world. The creative flow that emanates from this realm can replenish an individual's vital energy and support them in all their endeavors.

Exercise: Cherished Dream . . . or Fantasy?

1. Which of these interpretations currently resonates with you the most? This stage prompts you to consider these fundamental questions:
   What is your most cherished dream?
   What daily actions are you taking to transform that dream into reality?

2. Take a moment to reflect on the prevailing fantasies in your mind and the recurring life scenarios that occupy your thoughts.

ART THAT EVOKES THE SQUARE

- *Big Fish* (2003): This heartwarming film follows the life of Edward Bloom, a man known for his tall tales and vivid imagination. It celebrates the beauty of storytelling, fantasy, and the impact of one man's dreams on those around him.
- "The Yellow Wallpaper" by Charlotte Perkins Gilman: This short story delves into the disturbing effects of a woman's overactive imagination.

16
Dvesha
JEALOUSY

Expectations are resentments waiting to happen.

Anne Lamott

Dvesha represents a sense of repulsion or aversion to the elements of the real world, while jealousy emerges as a product of resentment fueled by unmet expectations. The latter occurs when the elaborate fantasies we've meticulously constructed collide with harsh reality, revealing a world in stark contrast to our grand mental designs. This gap between our lofty expectations and the somewhat capricious nature of reality can lead to profound disillusionment, shattering our belief in a predictable and reliable world.

What exacerbates this disconnect is the significant contrast between how we perceive ourselves and how others perceive us. We may have a grandiose view of ourselves, believing that we are nothing short of exceptional, but it becomes apparent that not everyone shares this sentiment. The disparity creates a sense of isolation, a feeling that no one truly understands our essence, and it is in this void that resentment takes root. In essence, jealousy is an act of defiance against reality, a firm disagreement between how the world treats us and how circumstances unfold. The disparity between our expectations and reality can exacerbate inner and outer conflicts.

Jealousy can lead us to impose our idealized vision on the outside world, deepening the conflicts we face. Individuals who feel pressured to conform to our expectations may eventually decide to break free of these shackles, leading to our self-imposed isolation from both society and the outside world. It's this isolation that leads us into the realm of greed.

Jealousy typically shifts our focus outward, away from our inner world, and fixates our attention on the lives of others, their choices, judgments, and expectations. On the journey of life, it's crucial not to be tied to the expectations of others. Giving up fragments of our essence and constantly seeking validation from others is a fruitless endeavor. It's essential to share love and cultivate friendships without expectation of return. Give because you wholeheartedly desire to, not in anticipation of receiving something in return.

Exercise: Attention and Solitude

Now take a moment for introspection: To whom do you give your undivided attention? Do you feel whole and content when solitude embraces you, or is there a lingering sense that something is amiss?

ART THAT EVOKES THE SQUARE

- *The Death of Sardanapalus* by Eugène Delacroix: This painting depicts the destruction of an Assyrian king's palace and his possessions, driven by jealousy and despair (1827, oil on canvas, Louve Museum, Paris).
- *The Age of Innocence* by Edith Wharton: This novel explores the jealousy and societal expectations within the upper class of New York during the Gilded Age.

To reconnect with our inner selves and refocus on what really matters, we must confront the snake that leads to Greed, square 4. This vital step forces us to ask ourselves the fundamental question, "What do I really want?" Rather than subjecting ourselves to endless comparisons or falling prey to envy and jealousy, we must instead explore our own desires and motivations.

17
Daya
COMPASSION

The more you know yourself, the more patience you have for what you see in others.

Erik Erikson

Daya, meaning compassion or empathy, represents the ability to truly understand and feel others, to see the world from their perspective. In this square a person realizes that those around them don't exist solely for their benefit or to cause them harm. Instead, they are just like the individual, seeking an end to suffering and the pursuit of happiness. Previously, there may have been fear, anger, demands, and expectations of others. But now there is a new level of understanding: People also experience pain and emotions.

Daya allows one to expand one's awareness and perception of others, even those who may have hurt one. Empathy is the genuine desire to understand why someone behaves the way they do, recognizing that everyone has valid reasons for their actions. Genuine forgiveness becomes possible when we truly understand the person and their motives, making it nearly impossible to harbor anger toward them.

Making conclusions based solely on our own experiences can lead to mistakes because we have blind spots in our perception. This stage encourages expanding our awareness through interactions with others and cultivating empathy.

Individuals no longer view others as adversaries; instead, they understand and sympathize with them. The heart is purified of anger and resentment. A deep understanding of the situation and the motives behind the behavior of others eliminates the need for resentment. In fact, individuals may even recognize their own role in causing others' pain.

In the state of compassion, individuals may encounter mental traps. The first is to become so absorbed in this wonderful feeling that they begin to suffer on behalf of others and lose touch with their own lives. The extreme form of this trap is the unconscious desire to see others remain unhappy and in pain. The second trap is the attempt to "save" the person for whom they feel compassion, sometimes with the intention of imposing their own ideas of what is right. This can lead to a path of violence. If you ever find yourself ensnared in one of these traps, I recommend revisiting the explanations of the Justice archetype found in the "Basic Archetypes" chapter of the book.

The attitude of this square can be summarized as "I understand you, but I retain my own perspective and opinions. I can see the world through your eyes, but I do not lose sight of my own vision."

Exercise: Forgiveness and Reconciliation

1. Read the story of Pope John Paul II who forgave his would-be assassin, Mehmet Ali Agca, after the 1981 assassination attempt. In a surprising move, the pope visited Agca in prison in 1983. Agca was later granted clemency and released from prison in 2000. This story exemplifies the power of forgiveness and reconciliation.
2. Write down three times when someone's behavior bothered you or seemed unfair. Think about what might have driven their actions—consider the social circumstances in which they grew up, whether they've experienced deep emotional wounds from their parents, or

whether they've struggled with feelings of abandonment. Now try to put yourself in their shoes, without resorting to the idea of "I would never have done that."

ART THAT EVOKES THE SQUARE

- *The Diary of Anne Frank* by Anne Frank: Anne's diary reflects the compassion and resilience of a young girl during the Holocaust as she seeks to understand the world and maintain her humanity.
- *To Kill a Mockingbird* by Harper Lee: This novel highlights the theme of compassion through the character of Atticus Finch, who demonstrates empathy and understanding in the face of prejudice and injustice.

This transformation brings an incredible sense of liberation and elevates us to the eighth level, to the square of the Absolute Plane (69), as compassion is considered a divine quality.

18
Harsha Loka
JOY

The meaning of life is to find your gift. The purpose of life is to give it away.

PABLO PICASSO

This state is like a soundtrack to the best moments of our lives. It's beautifully simple, yet deeply meaningful: "Joy is your compass on life's journey."

When you're in a state of joy, an incredible surge of energy flows through you, calling you to action. It's like a wellspring of enthusiasm that propels you forward. What's more, this is often where you get your "tools" for the road ahead—practical insights, creative ideas, and clear action plans.

The more joy you feel in your life, the more on track you are. Now, here's the catch with joy—it's all about the anticipation of action, not just the action itself. Think about the times you've bought a book brimming with excitement, only to let it gather dust on the shelf. Or when you signed up for a promising course but never found the time to complete it. In essence, joy is your catalyst for action, your boundless source of energy, and your assurance that you're on the right path in your life's journey.

Exercise: Invite More Joy

So it's time for some introspection. Ask yourself, "Am I experiencing enough joy in my daily life?" If not, what can you do to invite more of it into your world? What truly lights up your soul? And how well do you balance your responsibilities with the activities that simply make you happy?

ART THAT EVOKES THE SQUARE

- *Up* (2009): This animated film from Pixar, directed by Pete Docter, demonstrates the transformative power of joy in the face of adversity.
- *The Dance* by Henri Matisse: This painting captures the essence of joy through vibrant colors and fluid, dancing figures (1909–1910, oil on canvas, Museum of Modern Art, New York).

LEVEL 3
MIRRORING THE PSYCHE

On this level, individuals frequently base their decisions on their own intellectual reasoning rather than following the guidance of their heart or inner intuition. It's crucial to acknowledge that harboring certain doubts about one's intentions is a natural and integral aspect of self-discovery.

This stage is where one must navigate the intricacies of their life responsibilities. An imbalance in this area can give rise to two prevalent challenges. First, it may lead to evading responsibilities and adopting a victim mentality. Alternatively, it can result in an attempt to exert control or dominance over others to assert one's power.

Yet another formidable obstacle involves grappling with frustration. When frustration prevails, it can render a person inert, making them feel incapable of accomplishing anything. Parallel to the second level, it remains essential to align personal expectations with the realities of life. The key distinction here is that on the second level, expectations were directed at life, while on this level, the focus shifts inward, entailing expectations from oneself. These expectations have a significant impact on an individual's choices and overall well-being.

This phase primarily revolves around the quest for equilibrium between managing life's responsibilities and fulfilling one's self-expectations, all while embracing the constructive presence of doubt regarding one's intentions.

19
Karma
ACTION

Karma is not a punishment or reward but a reflection of your actions. It is your mirror.

Sadhguru

When people delve into the concept of karma, there's often a misconception about it being a form of cosmic retribution. However, the reality is far from the Universe's desire to punish. *Karma*, by definition, means "action." At this stage of the game, individuals come to realize that they define themselves through their actions. They understand that every action they undertake ripples through the world, creating echoes in the Universe, according to the law of karma. Humans are in perpetual interaction with the world; they are an integral part of it, not its adversary.

On the plane of karma, individuals accept responsibility for all their past, present, and future actions. They acknowledge that they, and only they, are responsible for the outcomes they face. Victimhood no longer holds any sway; victims are devoid of the power to act. Instead, individuals on this plane must cast aside their illusions, confront their reality, and accept it for what it is. This acceptance shouldn't be confused with complacency or inaction; rather, it's an acknowledgment that their present circumstances are the starting point for action, not a cause for lament.

Occasionally, a player may recognize their misguided actions and thoughts, yet they remain entrenched in old habits, unyielding in their strategies, or succumb to idleness. When this happens, the Game nudges them back down to the plane of karma. In some cases, players may evade responsibility and seek refuge in Bad Company (square 24), where their egos are nurtured and blame is shifted to external factors.

Should a player successfully navigate the plane of karma, they will be brimming with the desire to take action. Responsibility ceases to be a burden and instead becomes a wellspring of strength and freedom. Through their actions, they communicate their intentions, desires, and will to the world.

Exercise: Taking Action Today

What steps are you ready to take on your journey? What's on your agenda for tomorrow? What about today? What are you doing right now? Action serves as the conduit through which you breathe life into your true desires and shape the contours of your days ahead. In this very moment, you are shaping the world and the life you long for. Therefore, look within yourself and ask, "What actions must I take today to secure the world and life I desire tomorrow?"

ART THAT EVOKES THE SQUARE

- *Erin Brockovich* (2000): Based on a true story, this movie shows how one determined woman took action against a major utility company accused of polluting a small town's water supply.

20 Dana

CHARITY

Self-care is not selfish; you cannot serve from an empty vessel.

Eleanor Brown

Dana, a term derived from Sanskrit, teaches the profound meaning behind "charity" or "giving." But generosity must stem from capacity before it becomes virtue. You cannot offer breath if you are gasping for air. The ability to contribute, while still protecting your own resources, indicates a level of maturity, an understanding of self.

Still, giving feels good. It resonates with the soul. This arrow goes to the very essence of giving. When your actions benefit others, a sense of bliss envelops you. You may even feel a bit divine when you give to others. "I am good!" you think, and others perceive you as virtuous. Such experiences also feed the growth of the ego. These subtleties, if left unexamined, can easily go unnoticed because they're perfectly natural. There is no need to resist them by thinking, "It's not about me—I'm just doing good." Embrace it, accept yourself more, let your ego be satisfied and still stay connected to others. It's neither good nor bad; just observe—you're doing good and it satisfies your ego. And don't forget, a touch of self-deprecating humor can be appropriate.

There's a potential pitfall, however. A player may find immense pleasure in being virtuous, to the extent that they take on the role not out of a genuine desire to help, but to be seen as good, and to enjoy the feeling it gives them. Acts of charity can become a formality, or be done at the expense of oneself and one's loved ones. Take a moment to look around—those closest to you may need your support far more than strangers. Not because they are hungrier than the "kids in Africa," but because focusing on the larger needs of others may cause you to overlook the smaller needs of your own family.

Dana asks for more than intention—it asks for discernment. What are your motivations? Where is the line between generosity and self-neglect? Charity can serve as a training ground for your skills. It's the place where self-doubt and ambition find their balance. For some, it's the path to deeper passion and self-development. However, if fear and uncertainty overwhelm you, you may find yourself trapped in the realm of charity, working at a loss.

Exercise: The Act of Giving as a Reflection of You

What can you offer the world without depleting yourself? Do you feel an increase in your reservoir of energy as you give, especially in certain moments of action? These are the nuances that make the realm of Dana come alive, where the act of giving becomes a reflection of one's inner journey and self-discovery.

ART THAT EVOKES THE SQUARE

- *Les Misérables* by Victor Hugo: This classic novel tells the story of Jean Valjean, a man who shows great acts of charity and compassion, highlighting the transformative power of giving.
- *Pay It Forward* (2000): This film features a young boy who creates a system of goodwill where acts of charity are passed from one person to another.

Dana serves as the arrow that propels the player to square 32, Mahar Loka, the realm of the heart. This is where your heart expands as you engage in actions that bring happiness to others, fill you with joy, and cause your inner self to blossom.

21
Ksaman'Paap
REDEMPTION

Freedom is not worth having if it does not include the freedom to make mistakes.

MAHATMA GANDHI

In the previous stages, people often acted blindly, driven solely by their fears and desires. Unaware of the profound impact of their actions on life, they inadvertently caused harm to themselves and others. Successfully overcoming the karma plan brings a profound realization—the responsibility for their actions rests solely on their shoulders. They come to understand that they are the architects of their own problems. The Redemption square marks the point at which past mistakes are corrected, often accompanied by a profound sense of guilt for their past transgressions. Here, concealing one's guilt, either from oneself or from others, as a means of protecting a self-image of moral deficiency, is no longer an option. Instead, one must face one's guilt and take full responsibility for one's actions.

Occasionally, an individual's ego can play cunning tricks on them. If they can't be the paragon of goodness, they opt for the polar opposite and seek to be the embodiment of malevolence. The ego is indifferent to the direction of the inflation—whether it is the best or the worst—as long as it stands out as the ultimate. In such cases, individuals tend to blame themselves for the world's myriad ills. They become incessant apologists, a behavior that only exacerbates the irritation of those around them and further fuels their self-deprecation and compulsion to apologize.

Curiously, when players find themselves unable to deal with their guilt, they instinctively seek an escape. They seek out people who can absolve them, validate their moral virtue, and deflect blame onto others or external circumstances. This inevitably leads the individual into the dangerous realm of Bad Company (square 24), which ultimately results in a fall into Vanity (square 7).

In the realm of Redemption, it's imperative to gain insight from past experiences and use those lessons as a guide for the future to avoid repeating the same mistakes. Failure to do so perpetuates a cycle of anger, envy, and insignificance. Often, it takes time for the player to come to terms with and accept his imperfections after acknowledging his mistakes.

Occasionally, during the game, individuals may not be aware of the specific transgressions that require atonement. They may preemptively dread the process, anticipating it as a form of punishment. There's no need for such fear. If the game has brought someone to this stage, it means they won't escape this reality in the real world. When the time is right, the individual will realize exactly what needs to be corrected and will be eager to begin the process. Salvation, when embraced, always brings a sense of relief.

If you find yourself navigating life in repetitive circles or frequently facing identical situations, it indicates a lack of understanding on your part. Life subjects you to recurring scenarios precisely to facilitate your understanding of what requires transformation. Complex situations in life are often a reflection of lessons that need to be internalized. When properly understood, life ceases to create obstacles in your path.

Why does playing this game save years of human life? Because each time you move from one level to the next, you gain insight into the events of your existence. In the game, these revelations materialize in a matter of hours, whereas in reality they may take years to surface. Once these realizations come to light, you can free yourself from the cycle of repetitive situations. It's at this point that you will review your life experiences and consider how you might have handled those situations that remain in your memory as poorly handled. How could you have handled them differently?

Redemption offers a chance to transform yourself in every passing second, a platform to manifest your will and choices through your actions and reactions. With each passing moment, reality questions your intentions and how you intend to proceed on your path. By manifesting yourself differently, you are creating a new path.

Exercise: Choosing New Patterns

In what new ways are you willing to manifest, act, and think? What patterns recur in your life, and how might you choose to behave differently?

ART THAT EVOKES THE SQUARE

- *The Kite Runner* by Khaled Hosseini: This novel explores the themes of guilt and redemption through the story of Amir, who tries to atone for his past mistakes.

22

Dharma

LIVING IN HARMONY WITH YOURSELF

Your identity is what you do when no one is watching.

AMERICAN GANGSTER

The term *dharma* comes from Sanskrit and translates as "what is established and firm," "law," or "duty." In Vedic culture, it has a fundamental meaning, encapsulating a set of inherent norms and rules. For example, the dharma of water is to flow, while the dharma of fire is to burn. It defines the nature and purpose of something, outlining its core characteristics. In the same way, each person carries an invisible thread—a particular way of being, acting, offering—that the soul recognizes as true. The question is not "What do I want to do?" but rather "What am I meant to do?"

To live in harmony, one must recognize the dharma within oneself, which includes adhering to the laws dictated by one's physique, the dharma of the mind, the societal dharma that governs the community in which one lives, and the dharma of nature, which governs harmonious interactions with the natural world. Dharma thus encompasses the inner nature of the individual, the roles of society, and the overarching laws of life. Violating dharma disrupts both internal and external harmony.

It's important to distinguish between dharma and destiny. For example, the dharma of a hunting dog is speed, driven by its inherent nature to chase prey, while each particular dog may have its own unique destiny, such as bringing joy to its owner or protecting a child.

Upon reaching square 22, Dharma, one gains insight into one's own essence and understands what aligns with one's unique incarnation and circumstances. Acceptance of one's essence and societal laws is essential, as life experiences and ideal learning occur within these parameters. However, it's equally important to retain one's individuality and not become completely subsumed by one's dharma, as this can lead to becoming a mere cog in the social machine. It's important to recognize the relevance of dharma. There are instances where a person with a gentle nature may need to show strength and firmness.

Exercise: Aligning with Your True Self

So what is your dharma, your defining characteristic? The divine idea is to understand these qualities and align your life and aspirations accordingly. This approach fosters a more fulfilling, purposeful, and joyful existence. Each individual is unique, so how can you align your life and endeavors with your true self? What attributes of your soul and personality are you excited about developing as you progress along your life's journey?

ART THAT EVOKES THE SQUARE

- *Scream of the Ants* (2006): This is the most enigmatic film about India, portraying the country with raw realism rather than a veneer of mystique and fantasy. India, often seen as a mecca for truth seekers, starkly differs from glossy brochures. Instead of wise sages, there are deceitful charlatans preying on naive tourists. The sacred Ganges River is portrayed as an overflowing waste dump. Behind the tourist facade, India reveals its genuine spirituality and a reluctance to unveil its mysteries to newcomers. The film follows Iranian newlyweds, illustrating their contrasting beliefs and desires.

When you know your dharma, it's a lot easier to advance. You are going up to the Positivity square (60).

23
Swarga Loka
HEAVEN

We are what we repeatedly do. Excellence, then, is not an act, but a habit.

Aristotle

The square of Heaven (or "trust"), is at the core of the third level and serves as the nexus for all the lessons within this level. Here, the player envisions and creates their ideal life, a personal "paradise on Earth" free of negativity, anger, and suffering. Everything is created for pure joy, spiritual fulfillment, and harmony. When the player reaches this level, they are ready to manifest this vision, whether it's a heavenly haven within their family, or the desire to bring their business or society closer to this ideal. However, true needs are not revealed until the fourth row.

Confidence is a defining quality for players who reach this level, making them certain of their vision for happiness and believing in unending bliss within these circumstances. Here, the soul's drive for self-development intertwines with the ego's pursuit of pleasure and self-affirmation. Success at this level depends on their harmonious cooperation. However, there are potential obstacles to overcome.

First, overconfidence in one's vision of an ideal life can lead to detachment from reality, resulting in inappropriate actions. Second, the player may project their vision of paradise onto others, believing that everyone should adopt what he or she perceives as good or virtuous. This can lead to attempts to impose one's beliefs on others, even if well-intentioned, and can come across as coercive. Third, the ego can become inflated, fueled by a sense of infallibility and perfection, leading them to try to change others to conform to their views.

To overcome this level successfully, one must consciously and judiciously construct one's personal "paradise" while developing the willpower and courage to act. Ongoing self-evaluation is key to ensuring the ecological impact of one's actions on others, especially loved ones.

This level offers a unique opportunity for personal growth, self-discovery, and the realization of potential. It provides an inner sense of identity, purpose, and meaning. You become an active participant in manifesting yourself and observing how the world and life respond to your expressions. Your existence becomes meaningful to you, to those around you, and to the world at large. There is an innate belief that your presence on this Earth has meaning and serves a purpose.

Exercise: Purpose

Ask yourself one question, "What purpose do I serve?"

ART THAT EVOKES THE SQUARE

- *The Truman Show* (1998): This film directed by Peter Weir tells the story of a man living in what he believes is an ideal life but gradually realizes that it's a carefully constructed world. It explores themes of authenticity and the pursuit of an idealized existence.

24
Ku Sang Loka
BAD COMPANY

Show me your friends and I will show you your future.

JIM ROHN

Sanga refers to a community, and within it there is a negative community known as "Ku Sanga" or "bad company." At this level, the environment and the people around us become the determining factors in our development. If this environment is harmful, it leads the player into this metaphorical snake pit. An inflated ego plays a crucial role in attracting an environment of similarly inflated egos into the person's life. The individual seeks validation and self-worth through the company of those who reinforce his belief in his own goodness.

In such a negative community, the person becomes overly dependent on the opinions of others and ceases to engage in critical self-evaluation. Negative behaviors are often normalized or even celebrated, including actions such as drinking, cheating, looking down on others with "lower vibrations," or judging those with different beliefs. It can be challenging for the person to immediately recognize the life lessons intended for them in such an environment. Instead of introspection, the blame may be placed on others, labeling them as "bad" without recognizing their similarities.

Immersed in a state of bad company, individuals find it difficult to coexist harmoniously with the world. They create divisions, categorizing themselves as "good" and others as "bad." The primary goal becomes ego gratification and peer validation. As a person experiences personal satisfaction, they often become oblivious to actions that are not in accordance with their dharma, making it difficult to recognize their involvement in bad company.

Bad company often consists of individuals who, in the player's perception, are inferior or deserving of contempt. The defining characteristic of bad company is the player's growing belief in his superiority over others. Self-criticism is obscured by the influence of society. At this stage, the negative aspects of the person are prominently displayed, and the people within the community serve as mirrors reflecting the player's flaws. Awakened from the illusions of self-perfection and choice, the player must conduct a thorough self-analysis and work diligently to correct their mistakes.

Upon entering this level, you will be asked to evaluate your surroundings. Consider whether the people around you are contributing constructively to your journey toward the values you hold most dear. In particular, the same company that may be beneficial at one stage of your development may become detrimental at the next, as your values and priorities evolve. This isn't about labeling people as "bad," but rather recognizing that your paths, values, and developmental directions have diverged. Some people can be toxic to your growth.

Exercise: Hinderance on the Path to Growth

1. Analyze your environment, and consider these questions:
   Who refuses to accept you for who you are?
   Who is pressuring you to conform to someone else's image?
   Who hinders your personal growth?
   Who doesn't really see you for who you are?
   Who leaves you feeling drained after interacting with certain people?
2. Recognize that the symbolic snake leads you to square 7, Mada (Vanity), which is characterized by delusions of self, a condition born of being in the wrong company.

ART THAT EVOKES THE SQUARE

- *The Great Gatsby* by F. Scott Fitzgerald: This classic novel examines themes of vanity, false ideals, and the company one keeps. The characters are trapped in the pursuit of an illusion of the American Dream, surrounded by decadence and superficiality.

Square 24, Bad Company, leads you to rethink your surroundings; you are going down to square 7, Vanity.

25

Su Sang Loka
GOOD COMPANY

Surround yourself with those who lift you higher.

Oprah Winfrey

As one follows their dharma path, they naturally attract like-minded individuals into their life. These are the companions who share a common pursuit of personal growth and benevolent objectives. In this harmonious circle, the principle of synergy is at work, where the collective result far surpasses the sum of individual efforts. Consequently, rapid development becomes the norm for the player in such a supportive environment. Group members play a pivotal role in helping each other identify and overcome beliefs and behaviors that impede their progress, propelling them toward their full potential. Furthermore, they actively cultivate their finest qualities. Unlike in the previous square, Bad Company, where illusions about oneself and the world often thrive, in this square, Good Company, individuals collectively shed these illusions.

The role of having good company around us in our personal growth is absolutely crucial. Consider, for instance, someone whose current priority is financial prosperity. With whom should they associate? Wealthy individuals who have made significant progress in this domain. Through such associations, one gradually assimilates the attributes these individuals have honed in their pursuit. Similarly, if spiritual advancement takes precedence in a person's life, regardless of their current position on their path, they should seek companions they consider spiritually inclined. Yet, many avoid good company out of fear of comparison or inadequacy. But growth rarely happens in comfort.

At this level of the game, the level of the third chakra, the opportunity to make this choice arises: to embrace courage, humility, and the willingness to learn. Be careful that when you encounter people you aspire to emulate and grow with, the desire to embody their qualities does not become a subconscious challenge. This may lead to the unintentional creation of idols and the gradual loss of one's uniqueness and authentic self.

Being open and vulnerable, especially during a shared journey, is of paramount importance. True connection involves sharing one's experiences and listening without judgment or the need to seek approval. The quest for validation can be a stumbling block, often resulting in pushback. Crucially, both oneself and others should be allowed to make mistakes. An intriguing insight emerges: The person who serves as a catalyst for the player's growth need not necessarily be someone who is liked. Friendly and pleasant interactions do not guarantee mutual development. Conversely, a candid, sharp remark can trigger profound self-reflection. The game often reveals that individuals whom the player finds challenging can, in fact, be the catalysts for their growth.

How does one discern between being good company for each other and being detrimental to one another? It was once believed that competition among friends fostered growth. However, this approach can stifle individuality and uniqueness, which are crucial in positive company. The hallmark of this square, Good Company, is that it values shared goals and mutually respects each person's unique contributions. If there is competition or comparison in any aspect, the dynamics tend to revert to that of Bad Company. It is imperative to surround oneself with people who perceive and accept one's true self, acknowledging both their current state and untapped potential. Identifying these individuals amid the crowd and investing more time with them is essential.

Exercise: Seeking Out Good Company

Consider these two questions:

> Who among your current acquaintances embodies the essence of good company?
>
> Where can you seek out such companions?

ART THAT EVOKES THE SQUARE

- *Good Will Hunting* (1997): This movie tells the story of a young man's journey of self-discovery with the help of a mentor. It explores the positive influence of a guiding figure.

26
Dukha
SADNESS

> *There is no greater agony than bearing an untold story inside you.*
>
> Maya Angelou

Sadness embodies the depths of destructive and depressive states, signaling a disconnection from oneself and one's path. But what exactly is sadness? It's the struggle to accept present circumstances. Often, the player faces the challenge of accepting the harsh realities of life, such as the departure of a beloved person. Denial sets in, along with frustration with life and others. The "Why me?" and "Why them?" questions persist. When a piece of your life vanishes, a void emerges, and within that void, sadness takes form—a transformation of emptiness into something new. Refusing this transformation leads to denial, being closed-off, and perpetually dwelling in a particular moment of the past. So, where are you looking right now: backward, into the present, or forward into the future?

It's time to face the truth, and that truth often brings feelings of sadness. This sadness may come from the realization of human imperfection and the inability to help everyone. It may come from the understanding that the path to personal development is far from instantaneous, and that great mastery or immediate goal-achievement remains elusive. Sadness essentially embodies a sense of self-dissatisfaction. While greed also represents dissatisfaction, it differs in the sense that the person believes they require more to attain happiness. Sadness, on the other hand, arises when one has already made attempts to discover happiness but has failed. Either their achievements are disappointing, or they themselves are discouraged by their inability to find happiness. For those in a state of sadness, time seems to stand still, and the weight of their grief can feel endless. Vulnerability consumes them, making solitude a preferred refuge.

Remember, this state is temporary, but it has intrinsic value. It serves as a pause, a time to be with yourself, to reflect, to gather strength, and to move forward. Learning to experience sadness gracefully and tenderly is essential. It should be embraced in a warm and calm environment. Then, step by step, one can move forward, set new goals, and escape the clutches of lingering grief. Accept what has happened as reality and continue on your journey.

Exercise: Get to the Heart of Sadness

1. Write down one or more instances that evoke deep sadness in you. Get to the heart of these situations and try to identify what exactly is triggering this emotional response. In the case of the loss of a loved one, identify the elements you long for. Is it the cherished heart-to-heart conversations with your father, the cozy dinners at your mother's house, or the adventures you shared with a friend or partner that you miss dearly? What remains in your memory? Take time to articulate these feelings and consider ways to reconcile with them. Perhaps you will begin to organize warm get-togethers with friends or intellectual gatherings for like-minded people.

2. On the other hand, if you're unable to move on from a breakup with your partner and tend to avoid places or activities you once shared, it may be beneficial to visit these places and effectively reimagine the history associated with them. By doing so, you can alleviate pockets of resistance that are embedded in your subconscious. These pockets are often fueled by a desire to avoid encountering these places or people, for fear that revisiting them will lead to a relapse into the emotionally draining state you have struggled to overcome. Facing this resistance head-on can help you conserve a significant amount of your life's precious energy.

ART THAT EVOKES THE SQUARE

- *Manchester by the Sea* (2016): This film revolves around the lead character's overwhelming grief and guilt following a family tragedy. It offers a realistic portrayal of how one might grapple with profound sadness and depicts the importance of community and support.
- *A Little Life* by Hanya Yanagihara: This novel follows the lives of four friends, with one of them, Jude, carrying a tragic and deeply saddening past. It's a moving exploration of friendship, trauma, and the capacity for human resilience.

27
Param Artha
SELFLESS SERVICE

We rise by lifting others.

ROBERT INGERSOLL

When a person chooses to contribute to the betterment of the world on a daily basis, they enter the realm of service. Service is always characterized by selfless actions. Unlike charity, where one may perform good deeds occasionally or as a one-time act, here the player begins to engage in such acts consistently, as a natural part of their routine. In this square, Selfless Service, the individual doesn't seek rewards or approval from others; their actions are free of personal gain. They simply do what they feel is necessary. An essential aspect of service is the absence of sacrifice; even a hint of sacrifice in one's actions distinguishes it from true service.

This square takes the player to the fifth level of the game, to the Human Plane (square 41), where they realize their place among their fellow humans. Being part of a community, contributing to something greater than oneself, and offering what one can is the essence of service. It offers solace from loneliness and a sense of the meaninglessness of life. Yet it can be both an escape and a potential trap. The goal here is not to be good, but to be indispensable.

Proper goal-setting is critical to personal growth and development. A goal is what motivates a person to get out of bed in the morning and what they are willing to change themselves and their lives for. In this stage, individuals choose to dedicate their lives to something greater than their own existence. In the previous square, during the Sadness phase, individuals are focused on their inner world, preoccupied with their own problems. Shifting one's focus to someone or something else can be one of the most effective ways to combat depressive states.

What is your current goal? Remember that the higher the goal, the more you empower yourself. Strengths and resources are not simply given; higher energy is always sent for a specific purpose. In other words, when a person lives for something significant and meaningful, resources are provided to meet their basic needs and fulfill that purpose. The supreme goal of square 68 (Cosmic Consciousness) is an inner state that emphasizes the ability to look forward, whether in moments of sadness or joy. It gives you the motivation to keep moving forward. Even when your energy seems depleted and you've lost your inner compass, this square calls us back to what truly matters.

Exercise: The Goal of Service

1. This square invites you to consider the following: What is your ultimate goal? What drives you forward? It's a reminder to fulfill your responsibilities, even if they don't bring immediate pleasure. In such cases, if the player goes about the work without resistance, they may eventually reach the Agni Loka (Fire Plane, square 42), where they develop a growing interest in their tasks and acquires a taste for them.
2. Service brings inner peace. There is, however, one aspect that can cloud the purity of service: becoming too closely identified with one's tasks, merging with them. In this scenario, ask yourself, "What will I do when there's no one left to serve? When the children have grown up and moved on? When retirement beckons? Who will I be then?"

ART THAT EVOKES THE SQUARE

- *The Blind Side* (2009): This movie portrays the real-life story of Leigh Anne Tuohy, who opens her home and heart to a homeless teenager, Michael Oher, and helps him fulfill his potential.
- *Hotel Rwanda* (2004): This movie is based on the true story of Paul Rusesabagina, a hotel manager who sheltered and saved the lives of over a thousand refugees during the Rwandan genocide.

The Selfless Service square (27) marks the culmination of the third level of the game and leads the player to the fifth level, characterized by the fundamental desires for self-expression and self-realization, to the square of Human Plane (41).

LEVEL 4

REVEALING HIGHER INTUITION

On the fourth level of the game, the player endeavors to strike a harmonious balance between the spiritual and physical aspects of their being. This stage is marked by a profound realization that one's existence extends beyond the confines of the physical body and the knowledge already acquired. It is at this point that the focus shifts to the heart center.

In this phase, the player embarks on a transformative journey aimed at purifying and mending the heart. The goal is to develop the ability to listen to one's heart, which, in turn, awakens intuition and heightened sensitivity. It's important to note that when grief overwhelms the player, it can lead to the closure of the heart.

To navigate this challenge, a deliberate choice is required to delve into the origins of this grief, comprehending the when and why behind the heart's emotional wounds. By undertaking this introspective process, the player can begin to reestablish a profound connection with their heart, tapping into its invaluable wisdom and guidance.

28

Sudharma

CONFIDENCE

Be yourself; everyone else is already taken.

OSCAR WILDE

Sudharma is your unique dharma, your inherent nature, and most importantly, the acceptance and revelation of your authentic self. It's the state in which you realize that you have the perfect qualities to fulfill your purpose. Dharma is a gift, the qualities and talents given to you at birth, which are unchangeable and not meant to be changed. However, how you choose to use these inherent qualities is your personal choice. The arrow of Sudharma represents the moment when you take control of your life. This life is entirely yours, with all its ups and downs. When you look back on your life, you can exclaim, "What a wonderful life I've had! I've had a remarkable journey on Earth with incredible people." This means you are on the right path.

The mind is always loud and demanding, but the heart whispers softly and only once, so it's crucial to listen to it. Trusting it and venturing into the unknown, even if it's intimidating, is vital. It's like a banker quitting his job to pursue his lifelong passion. The path of the heart doesn't promise eternal happiness or the absence of obstacles. In fact, it's a challenging path to follow, filled with trials and hurdles. The pitfall of this stage is the lack of critical analysis. The heart rules more than the mind, and its impulses aren't always rational. Failure to navigate this "heart" phase could mean never achieving a balance between heart and mind. Rushing headlong into following the heart without due consideration can lead to results very different from those desired. Fear of repeated setbacks and difficulties can close the heart and cause the player to deviate from the path.

Exercise: Manifest Your Unique Self

Write down three facets of your unique self. How could you manifest them?

ART THAT EVOKES THE SQUARE

- *Whale Rider* (2002): This film tells the story of a young Maori girl who challenges her community's traditions to fulfill her destiny and follow her sudharma.

The arrow from square 28 will take you to Tapa Loka (Austerity, square 50), where your priorities are aligned with your soul's desires. To reach this level, you must embrace what you have and how it has been given to you in this moment, and you must listen to the wisdom of your heart. It's a time to embrace and reveal your true essence.

29

Adharma
BLIND FAITH

> *Commit not a single unwholesome action, cultivate a wealth of virtue, to completely tame this mind of ours, this is the teaching of the Buddhas.*
>
> SCOTT TUSA

When you are aligned with your dharma, as in the last square, the entire Universe supports you; however, when you stray into Adharma, square 29, you must rely solely on your own determination and strength.

The prefix *a* is a negation, which essentially means "no." Dharma encompasses your true essence and nature. When you encounter square

6, Attachments, on the path, it serves as a signal to pause and reevaluate your current direction, as well as the rules and beliefs you've accepted. Adharma reflects the tension between inner truth and external conformity. This often happens when fear closes the heart, eroding trust and allowing the mind to take control despite its inherent limitations. But conflict can be fertile. It can break old patterns and shape new spaces that reflect your true potential. Don't fear the friction. It's where new realities begin.

Exercise: Life Assessment

At this point, it's crucial to do a thorough life assessment. You should question your relationships and your field of activity:

"Do I still want to be with this person?"

"Is what I'm doing now in line with my desires? Can I see and maintain interest in personal growth?"

ART THAT EVOKES THE SQUARE

- *Self-Portrait with Cropped Hair* by Frida Kahlo: This iconic self-portrait by Kahlo captures her defiance and courage in the face of societal expectations and explores themes of identity and self-acceptance (1940, oil on canvas, private collection).
- *The Stranger* by Albert Camus: This existential novel portrays the life of Meursault, a detached and apathetic man who embodies the fear of confronting one's inner emotions and desires.

The snake here represents unrealized potential and serves as a symbol that prompts us to examine our limiting beliefs. Pursuing a path that isn't truly yours will ultimately prove unfulfilling. If you find yourself drained of energy, it's time to make a change. You are moving down the snake to the square of Attachments (6).

30

Uttama Gati
GOOD TENDENCIES

The aim of life is to achieve happiness, and the means of achieving it is through self-discipline.

HARISH JOHARI

Uttama Gati means noble movement—the path of conscious growth. What is worth investing resources in means something different for each person, but many follow inherited scripts—school, career, family—without questioning whether those choices reflect inner truth or are shaped by external influence. Nietzsche wrote, "Become who you are." Growth isn't about perfection—but choosing a path that reflects your desires and ultimately deepens you.

Exercise: Your Correct Intentions

What thoughts did you have when you landed in this square? Falling into it emphasizes the correctness of your intentions—you are on the right path!

ART THAT EVOKES THE SQUARE

- *Two Lives* by Concordia Antarova: One of my favorite books, and incomparable in depth, this book is a coming of age story of 17-year-old Lyovushka as he navigates relationships, unexpected adventures, and spirituality. Antarova's work ultimately focuses on positivity and calm in approaching challenges.
- *Mr. Nobody* (2009): This movie examines the life—and approaching death—of Nemo, the last mortal on Earth. He is able to view multiple potential outcomes of his life's choices, with his storytelling constantly shifting as a result.

31
Yaksha Loka
SANCTUARY

There are two ways to live your life. One is as though nothing is a miracle. The other is as though everything is a miracle.

Albert Einstein

The Sanctuary square is not merely a place of rest—it is the crossing point where you connect with your *inner master*, your guiding light in life. This inner guide is ever present, offering clarity on your path and the best course of action. When you stand within this square, you can turn to your inner teacher and pose the questions: What knowledge do you seek? What understanding do you lack?

When you embrace change and growth, the world accelerates its transformative processes. In moments of uncertainty or when questions arise, simply close your eyes and seek guidance. The answers will unfailingly manifest: through people, literature, the vast cosmos, or symbolic signs. But you must be willing to hear what is true, not just what is easy. Alignment, even when uncomfortable, is more valuable than certainty.

Exercise: A Question for Your Inner Master

What is the question you would like to ask your inner master?

ART THAT EVOKES THE SQUARE

- *The Celestine Prophecy* by James Redfield: The book and its film adaptation revolve around a journey to find and understand a set of ancient spiritual insights, where the characters meet various guides and mentors.

- *Peaceful Warrior* (2006): This film, based on Dan Millman's autobiography, depicts the author's journey from a college gymnast to meeting an enigmatic gas station attendant who becomes his spiritual mentor.

32
Mahar Loka
BALANCE

The truth is balance. However the opposite of truth, which is unbalance, may not be a lie.

Susan Sontag

Mahar Loka (Balance), embodies the fourth energy center, a threshold beyond the familiar dramas of the ego. It is associated with the anahata chakra, which is closely connected to the level of our consciousness and the corresponding experiences we encounter in life. At the initial stage, represented by the first chakra, the idea of reaching this level may not even be considered, for to dwell here, one must first meet the shadow—not to exile it, but to integrate it.

Once you recognize the parts of yourself that fear silence, cling to praise, and resist sorrow, you begin to soften their hold. This makes space for the full spectrum of life in all its vibrant colors, shades, dimensions, and complexities. It's a state of profound harmony and equilibrium where the heart opens, giving rise to wondrous occurrences. This openhearted state is one of the most profound experiences attainable while in a physical body. An open heart emits love, and it naturally draws animals and beings toward the person. The heart remains open as long as one remains authentic, only closing when one conforms to self-imposed boundaries.

This state is all about the capacity to authentically integrate and express your true self in the world. Balance is not stillness, but alignment—the ongoing capacity to return to yourself, even when the world sways. Your task is to know what brings you back, and to choose it—again and again.

Exercise: Inner Harmony

For those who have arrived at this level via the Charity arrow (Dana, square 20) it's essential to ask yourself, "What am I willing to relinquish, knowing that it does not contribute to the balance in my life? What do I currently lack in order to attain inner harmony? Why?"

ART THAT EVOKES THE SQUARE

- "Here Comes the Sun" by the Beatles: This song by George Harrison reflects the arrival of brighter days and a sense of balance, offering hope and renewal.

33
Gandha Loka
FRAGRANCE

> *Smell is a potent wizard that transports us across thousands of miles and all the years we have lived.*
>
> Helen Keller

This square marks the refinement of our perception. It's where we start to discern subtle aromas, tune in to people's thoughts and intentions, and anticipate their next moves. What does this encounter or proposition smell like? Trust your sense of smell, trust your instincts. If you encounter someone or something that feels unpleasant, be honest with yourself about your feelings and act accordingly.

Embrace the ability to sense the subtle, to listen beyond the tangible world. Your soul communicates through the ethereal, and your sensory organs guide you on the right path. It's crucial for your intuition to translate into action, so learning to trust yourself is essential. The mind often provides logic, external knowledge, and foreign experiences, but may cause you to doubt and seek validation for your choices. The opinions of others, as if they know better, can be a helpful resource. Holding on to rigid beliefs can hinder this capacity.

Exercise: Trusting Your Sense of Scent

Consider the following questions:

What doesn't sit well in your life?

What scents draw you in?

Are you overly reliant on others' opinions when making decisions?

ART THAT EVOKES THE SQUARE

- *Ratatouille* (2007): This animated film from Pixar explores the world of fine dining through a rat named Remy who has an exceptional sense of smell and taste. It highlights how smells and flavors can evoke memories and emotions.

34 Rasa Loka TASTE

All of life is a dispute over taste and tasting.

FRIEDRICH NIETZSCHE

In this square, the focus shifts from intuition and prediction to full engagement in our activities and interactions, and the experience of the present moment. Here, you are encouraged to trust your senses on a deeper level. You are not just what you eat—you are what you absorb, what you allow in. Each input shapes your inner world. You develop a keen sense of what is nourishing and what is detrimental to your well-being. Your senses act as a compass to help you navigate through life. Taste becomes a spiritual ethic, not a matter of elitism but of care. Cultivation—rather than consumption—teaches the soul to recognize quality.

Exercise: Refining Your Palate

How can you refine your palate? Perhaps consider taking a break from salt and spices to truly savor the natural flavors of food. Over time, you might find that the urge to sweeten or spice up your relationships with others diminishes because the genuine connection will be satisfying on its own.

ART THAT EVOKES THE SQUARE

- *The Particular Sadness of Lemon Cake* by Aimee Bender: In this book, the protagonist can taste the emotions of the people who prepare the food she eats. This unique sensory experience adds a layer of complexity to her understanding of the people in her life.
- *Like Water for Chocolate* (1992): This film is another well-known example of emotions being tied to food.

35
Naraka Loka
PURGATORY

The phoenix must burn to emerge.

JANET FITCH

Purgatory serves as the crucible of transformation, a realm immersed in turmoil when the subtler dimensions become tainted. It acts as the chamber for refining these subtle planes. Oftentimes, this process is initiated by severe illness, the loss of beloved individuals, or events that trigger the obliteration of structures painstakingly constructed over the years. It is through pain and moments of upheaval that values are subjected to a thorough reevaluation, and one's consciousness and perception of reality undergo a profound reprogramming. This purification process extends to the elimination of erroneous beliefs and the deconstruction of entrenched thought patterns. Layers of identity that have outlived their utility are shed, leaving the individual feeling lighter, liberated from the shackles of past memories, emotions, and melancholy. The road forward becomes visible. But where does it lead to?

In this state, conventional modes of behavior and action no longer suffice, yet a comprehensive understanding of the future remains elusive. It's a realm of uncertainty, where there is no turning back, yet the path ahead is shrouded in mystery. It is a pivotal point, and once traversed, it propels us toward the next phase of our personal development. Pain, in its essence, becomes an agent of purification. Embracing it rather than recoiling from it is crucial. Through painful ordeals, we gain insights and are guided toward a higher purpose. When the reasons behind enduring this state are revealed, we become not embittered but grateful, setting forth with renewed purpose.

In our quest to free ourselves from the constraints that hinder our true selves, we may find ourselves shedding tears, struggling with resistance, and confronting uncomfortable emotions. This is an inherent part of any practice dedicated to self-liberation and self-purification. However, it is far more beneficial to confront this pain in the context of a practice of our own choosing rather than to allow it to manifest as challenging life events. By consciously purifying ourselves, we facilitate a more effortless and enjoyable journey along our chosen path. Take, for example, the practice of nail standing, which offers both physical and energetic cleansing by targeting specific biologically active points on the feet.

Stimulating these points triggers the immune system and initiates a comprehensive reset, inducing a state of relaxation and vitality. At the same time, our consciousness expands, and a reservoir of energy is unleashed. As we stand on these nails and endure the intense pain in our feet, we unearth the strength to express gratitude for the pain and the many blessings that life bestows upon us.

Exercise: Purification Through Catharsis

Engage in practices that purify your body through catharsis. This can be similar to the practice of nail standing through the activation of pressure points. Another example one could try would be a candle meditation practice, which has Hindu origins. After a long workday, you can come home, sit in a dark room, and focus on five to twenty candles. This practice often brings about tears, initiating a cleansing process. It's particularly beneficial for people who tend to block their emotions or have chosen to suppress them because life feels safer without them.

ART THAT EVOKES THE SQUARE

- *Crimes of the Future* (2022): This film directed by David Cronenberg explores a futuristic world where biotechnological advancements have eliminated physical pain for the majority of the population.

36

Swatccha

CLARITY OF CONSCIENCE

Clarity is the counterbalance of profound thoughts.

Luc de Clapiers

Clarity of Conscience is a state of nonjudgment, a world without black and white distinctions. Doubts and the burdensome weight of decisions disappear. This is liberation. Your consciousness remains clear and untainted, a pristine window to the world. You see reality as it is, guided by your soul and spirit, walking hand in hand. Your identity and the roles of others become clear, and life's priorities (health, family, love, work) are in focus.

Exercise: Questions for Clarity

While enjoying this state of clarity, answer these questions:

In which areas are you already fulfilled?

In which areas do you need to pay attention?

ART THAT EVOKES THE SQUARE

- "Fields of Gold" and "Fragile" by Sting: These songs reflect the clarity of love and nostalgia, as the singer recalls a past relationship with a sense of fondness and timelessness.

LEVEL 5

MANAGING YOUR VITAL ENERGY

As one progresses toward the fifth level, the focus shifts to the pursuit of self-realization, where the individual embarks on a quest to understand their role in society, to find their niche among their peers, and to cultivate their distinct identity. The key lies in mastering the art of self-expression and honing the ability to engage with others on verbal and energetic levels.

To successfully navigate this path, one must confront and overcome numerous societal pressures and exhortations. Messages such as "conform to the norm," "fit in," "emulate the success of your peers," and "don't challenge the system, embrace the status quo" are part of the social machinery's arsenal. These directives not only restrict our cognitive freedom but also shackle us, stifling our creative impulses, fostering self-doubt, and constantly instigating comparisons with our peers. An unrestrained and independent personality is perceived as a threat to the system, resistant to manipulation or control.

In this stage, individuals come to know their own unique identity, unearth their spiritual essence, and delve into their multifaceted potential. Participants gain access to the Supreme Library of Knowledge, a repository of universal wisdom providing direct, unmediated insights into the vast tapestry of human understanding. As a result, they gain the prerogative to express their thoughts, share their viewpoints, and resonate in this world. However, it's imperative to note that those who abuse this privilege to spread falsehoods or deceive others may face challenges and obstacles on their journey at this stage.

37

Jnana

WISDOM

It is the mark of an educated mind to be able to entertain a thought without accepting it.

Aristotle

What is wisdom? It's not the product of reading countless books or acquiring textbook knowledge; rather, it's the profound wisdom that life imparts. Jnana, true knowledge, embodies enlightenment and insight. Imagine a person navigating a labyrinth, looking for patterns and an escape route. Then, suddenly, they're given a bird's-eye view of the labyrinth and everything becomes clear. Through personal experience, one begins to fathom the core of existence. While situations may seem negative from a personal perspective, from the perspective of the soul, clarity emerges: There is no injustice, no death, no betrayal. All conflict is at the level of personality and ego. This is the essence of jnana—a state that welcomes revelations and realizations, perceives causes and consequences, understands the laws of karma, and revels in the blissful understanding of life.

However, it's a misconception to believe that everything will now be effortless and uncomplicated. The Universe is constantly offering lessons to ensure our continued growth. A player who has deciphered his first "maze" may expect a smoother path, but a new maze awaits.

Exercise: Contemplate Wisdom

Contemplate this state of wisdom and try to remember it. There is nothing else to do.

ART THAT EVOKES THE SQUARE

- *The Man from Earth* (2007): This is a thought-provoking film centered around a character who has lived for thousands of years and shares his wisdom.

The wisdom lifts you up to the square of Bliss (66).

38
Prana Loka
VITAL IMPULSE

Everything is energy, and that's all there is to it. Match the frequency of the reality you want, and you cannot help but get that reality.

ALBERT EINSTEIN

One of the core skills a person can develop is the ability to harness their own energy and employ practices that gradually expand their energetic capacity. These practices are vital for unleashing one's full potential, as realizing one's capabilities often demands a considerable amount of energy. Think of your body as a vessel, akin to a glass that can initially hold only 250 milliliters of water. Yet, you aspire to pour in a full liter, representing numerous projects and greater financial success. What occurs in such a scenario? Spillage and wastage. Similarly, if your energy capacity remains limited, you might find yourself overwhelmed by financial opportunities and unable to effectively manage the projects that come your way, potentially leading to stress or burnout.

To enhance your energetic capacity, various practices are available, such as breathing exercises, meditation, daily journaling (this practice is ideal for meditation preparation; see the exercise on p. 185), and physical activities, among many others. These practices gradually increase your energy-holding capabilities, helping you better manage the abundance of opportunities and resources. There are myriad breathing techniques to help you connect with your vital impulse and energy. Look up practices such as diaphragmatic breathing, hyperventilation, sudarshan kriya, or pranayama. It will be great if you have the opportunity to explore one of these practices in person and feel the effects on your body. If, for one circumstance or another, you are unable to go to a master who will guide you on breathing techniques, discover a basic breathing practice online.

A popular yogi breathing exercise is called *pranayama* and is ideal for this kind of energy work. The Sanskrit word can be separated into two parts, *prana* and *ayama*, which can be translated as "life force" and "length, stretch, hold" respectively. Yogis believe that prana is present in the air, yet is neither oxygen nor nitrogen. Prana permeates our entire body. It supports all the functions of the body, because the air currents moving through the energy channels, which are invisible to ordinary vision, are the energies of the subtle human body and are controlled by pranayama techniques. Breath control is the tool with the help of which the practitioner begins to realize prana and how it is manifested in various external and internal processes.

Additionally, it's not just about expanding capacity; it's also about the quality of the energy you absorb. This doesn't pertain solely to the quality of your diet but extends to the ecological manner in which you acquire energy from your surroundings. If you've been inadvertently sustaining yourself through negative energies like conflicts, complaints, or passive-aggressive behavior, you might not realize that such energy isn't nourishing your growth but is, in fact, detrimental to your well-being.

In the following exercise, I will describe pranayama; however, I am not an expert on breathing practices. You are welcome and encouraged to open an internet video that you align with and do any basic breathing exercise before moving on with the game.

Exercise: Pranayama Breathing

1. Preparation
   - Maintain proper body posture when performing breathing practices.

   When you are doing breathing exercises, you should remember that your body should be in the most comfortable position possible throughout the practice. If you are unfamiliar with *padmasana* (lotus pose), sit in any comfortable cross-legged meditative pose. You should always keep your back upright throughout your practice.

   - The chest should be open, shoulders straightened to breathe fully. When breathing, the chin is picked up and the top of the head is pulled up.
   - If you feel tightness in the pelvis or discomfort in the lumbar region, you can sit on a blanket (fold it two or three times so that the pelvis is higher than the feet). In this way you will be able to keep your spine in an upright position.

   Any discomfort in the body is inadmissible, as the essence of the process is lost; all your attention will be directed to the area of discomfort, and therefore you will not be able to concentrate on the internal processes.

2. Be aware of the proportion of inhalation and exhalation.

   In pranayama practice and beyond, it is recommended to pay great attention to inhalation and exhalation. Smooth exhalation should be approximately twice as long as inhalation. For example, if the inhalation lasts seven seconds, then the exhalation should last fourteen seconds. This principle is necessary in order to fully empty the lungs and perform the subsequent full breath.

3. Practice the *anuloma viloma* (alternate nostril) pranayama technique.
   - Place the thumb of your right hand on the outside of your right nostril, fold your pointer and middle finger out of the way, and place your ring finger on the outside of your left nostril.
   - Inhale through the right nostril for seven counts, then gently press down with your thumb to close your right nostril.
   - Exhale through your left nostril for fourteen counts.

- Inhale through your left nostril for seven counts.
- Gently press down with your ring finger to close your left nostril.
- Exhale through your right nostril for fourteen counts, then inhale for seven counts.
- Do twelve repetitions, with time increasing to twenty-four cycles.

ART THAT EVOKES THE SQUARE

A mantra meditation (guiding chant) focusing on the seven chakras will evoke this square. Check YouTube or other social media platforms to find one that suits you.

39
Apana Loka
ELIMINATION

Letting go is freedom. Holding on is suffocation.

THICH NHAT HANH

Apana, according to Hindu philosophy, is one of the five vital energies described in the Vedic texts, each serving a specific role in our bodies. Apana, in particular, is the downward-moving energy responsible for elimination processes like defecation and urination, as well as the body's purification. It plays a vital role in ridding the body of physical waste products.

Maintaining a well-functioning elimination system is crucial. When issues arise, a body cleanse can be beneficial. You might consider dedicating one day a week to fasting, giving your organs a break from constant food digestion. A weekly fasting day is not overly challenging but can have significant benefits for your physical well-being.

This concept extends to the spiritual realm as well. Just as you must keep your body's elimination processes in order, you should also release unnecessary connections and responsibilities that drain your energy. It's essential to let go of burdens that no longer serve you, even if you feel solely responsible for them. By releasing what holds you back, you can take the next step on your path.

Exercise: Ready to Release

Embracing this square reminds you of the importance of shedding what no longer aligns with your journey. What are you ready to release now? What is hindering your progress?

ART THAT EVOKES THE SQUARE

- *The Whale* (2022): This American drama, directed by Darren Aronofsky, is about Charlie, a reclusive online English writing instructor living with morbid obesity. He teaches college students through a faceless webcam, hiding his shame about his physical appearance. His only confidante, Liz, a compassionate nurse, persistently encourages him to confront his health issues, including congestive heart failure, while he navigates the challenging process of eliminating both physical toxins and emotional baggage.

40

Vyana Loka

CIRCULATION

> *Energy cannot be created or destroyed, it can only be changed from one form to another.*
>
> Albert Einstein

Prana, the energy entering the human body, and *apana*, the energy leaving it, are essential components. *Vyana*, however, is the subtle energy that surrounds and circulates within the human being, often referred to as the *aura*. This life force orchestrates bodily functions such as the heartbeat, blood circulation, lymphatic flow, glandular activity, and oxygen distribution to each cell. It's responsible for the movement of blood through the capillaries and the regulation of perspiration. Vyana essentially maintains the harmony of our internal environment.

In square 38, Prana emphasizes the importance of expanding our energetic capacity through various practices. In Vyana Loka, however, we delve into the need to protect ourselves from energy leaks. Increasing our energy levels without sealing these leaks can inadvertently deplete our reserves. Therefore, it becomes imperative to address and eliminate these energy leaks. These leaks can take many forms, such as individuals who drain our energy, the compulsion to solve everyone's problems, excessive involvement in other people's affairs, manipulative behaviors that make us vulnerable, or working solely for monetary gain. The first step is to plug these energetic voids to prevent further loss.

As we work intensely and mindfully on vyana within ourselves, we increase our energetic integrity. This process involves redirecting our focus and resources back to our own well-being. We stop solving other people's problems for them to solve on their own and regain control of our own lives. It's similar to refocusing our attention on self-care.

Exercise: Energy Drains

No matter how much we fill ourselves, these leaks, if left unaddressed, will continue to drain our energy. It's imperative to diagnose and identify the points of energy leakage in your life. What is the source of your energy drain?

ART THAT EVOKES THE SQUARE

- *Infinity Mirrored Room* by Yayoi Kusama: These immersive art installations have been presented in various forms and locations since the 1960s. Each installation is a small, mirrored space filled with hundreds of LED lights that pulse in different colors, creating the illusion of infinite depth and blending the viewer into a boundless, interconnected Universe. The installation evokes the flow of energy within the self and the cosmos, mirroring how vyana loka integrates and harmonizes the energies of prana and apana. It invites reflection on protecting and balancing our energy fields, emphasizing the importance of sealing energetic leaks to maintain internal harmony and vitality.

41
Jana Loka
HUMAN PLANE

The cave you fear to enter holds the treasure you seek.

JOSEPH CAMPBELL

Who are you? There is a unique flow within you, something you can do effortlessly, regardless of your age, state of mind, or external rewards. It's your authentic expression and the key to your fulfillment.

If one's pursuit of fulfillment revolves solely around financial gain, it may not always reveal one's true beauty or talents. True self-actualization comes from a deep desire, an irresistible calling, rather than manipulative attempts to barter with the Universe for money or recognition.

However, this stage can also apply to our interactions with others and society. In the previous phase, the player discovered the Divine within. Now they strive to recognize the Divine in others, fostering mutual respect and authentic communication. At square 41, Human Plane, the player no longer relies solely on external guidance. They understand that their personal experience is of greater importance. They respect the experiences of others without imposing their own. In this realm, they engage with others as equals and find their unique place in society.

A notable aspect of this state is the player's reduced participation in training, seminars, and transformational events. Their lives become simpler, focusing on daily routines and tasks. This simplicity and tranquility provides the necessary cocoon for an "inner butterfly transformation." Successfully navigating the challenges of the Human Plane allows the player to authentically express themselves in society and enjoy interpersonal relationships. The player explores different roles and enjoys how others express themselves.

A common pitfall at this stage is to become overly identified with the social role one plays, losing one's authentic self in the process. Fulfillment at this stage comes not from becoming someone new, but from becoming open for something greater to move through you, toward others.

Exercise: Deepen Your Fulfillment

What does fulfillment mean to you right now? Where in your life do you long for deeper self-actualization? These questions contain valuable insights.

ART THAT EVOKES THE SQUARE

- *Brave New World* by Aldous Huxley: In this dystopian novel, the society's pursuit of pleasure and consumerism leads to a loss of individuality and true fulfillment. The characters grapple with their desires in a world that prioritizes superficial happiness over genuine connection and authenticity.

42 Agni Loka FIRE

Life is a pure flame and we live by the invisible sun within us.

Thomas Browne

Within each of us is a divine spark, a flicker of sacred fire. This inner flame is our life force, and when we enter square 42, Agni Loka, it burns even brighter. Here we rekindle our connection to the Divine and recognize our part in the grand tapestry of existence. In this state, fear disappears and we are driven to live and express ourselves without reservation. The level of Agni gives us the freedom to be our true selves, to create our own destiny and to attract opportunities. The only caution is not to let this fire consume us.

Fire is the agent of rapid change, and Agni Loka is the realm of rapid transformation. If you are prepared for rapid metamorphosis, the Universe will grant you the speed to progress on your journey without losing your way. The Cosmos knows when the time is right to accelerate change, helping you to rid yourself of obstacles while preserving what can be refined and improved.

Agni Loka is the energy of transformation. Just as a fire reduces everything to ashes, it wipes the slate clean and erases old forms.

Exercise: The Fire of Transformation

1. Consider the following: What new form matches your current state? What aspects of your life need to be transformed right now? You can change the way you react to certain situations, learn to master your emotions, and even revolutionize your relationships.
2. In the coming days, make it a point to spend some time by the fire. Observe the flames dancing and consider the significance of fire. What do you associate with it? What insights might you gain from this elemental presence? Is its meaning solely about transformation? The Universe has scattered clues everywhere, you just have to pay a little more attention.

ART THAT EVOKES THE SQUARE

- *Firestarter* (1984): Based on Stephen King's novel, this film follows a young girl with pyrokinetic abilities and explores the dangerous power of fire.

43

Janma
SECOND BIRTH

No bird soars too high if he soars with his own wings.

William Blake

Janma means "birth." A person's birth is not only a significant event in the game but also a pivotal milestone in life. In this journey, much like in the real world, a person experiences two distinct births. The first marks their physical entry into this world, while the second marks the birth of their unique personality.

This stage becomes relevant when a player is ready to break free from societal constraints and the compulsion to conform to the norms and expectations set by others. It's a phase of self-acceptance, embracing one's individuality, and shedding the role of being a mere cog in the social machine. People are often grouped or categorized based on various characteristics such as gender, occupation, or social roles, but personality defies such categorization; it is singular and genuine.

At this point, individuals renounce predetermined social roles, religious affiliations, and class distinctions. They allow their authentic thoughts, emotions, and behaviors to flourish. They can no longer be neatly pigeonholed, and the pursuit of approval from others loses its appeal. While they may have once craved approval and to stand out, a fully formed personality finds that such validation is no longer a necessity.

This stage of awakening and self-recognition comes with a deep understanding of life's purpose, goals, and priorities for this incarnation, and the ideal time for their realization. Self-awareness brings a newfound appreciation for time, arguably life's most precious resource. Time is valued and its expenditure on trivial matters is minimized.

Exercise: Making the Most of Your Time

The purpose of life becomes clearer, prompting the individual to ask, "Why did I come into this world, and how can I make the most of the time the Universe has given me?"

ART THAT EVOKES THE SQUARE

- *Fight Club* (1998): Directed by David Fincher and based on Chuck Palahniuk's novel, this film delves into the themes of identity and self-discovery. The main character, known as the Narrator, undergoes a process of rebirth, which can be seen as a symbolic second birth. Through his alter ego, Tyler Durden, he questions societal norms and conformity, and rejects the established order in favor of seeking one's true self and purpose, ultimately leading to the birth of a new, unconventional personality.

44
Avidya
IGNORANCE

> *The greatest enemy of knowledge is not ignorance, it is the illusion of knowledge.*
>
> Stephen Hawking

A serves as a negative prefix, much like the absence of light in darkness. *Vidya,* on the other hand, means "knowledge." Avidya, therefore, is akin to the embodiment of ignorance squared. The snake that bites here doesn't just drag you downward; it pulls you inward, away from your feelings and into the trap of overthinking.

As your personal evolution progresses, you earnestly hope to free yourself from the shackles of "terrible" experiences. You have gone through numerous lessons, realizing that in the grand scheme of things, right and wrong are mere constructs, and it's your perspective that truly matters. You have honed the art of accepting your past and tending to your emotional wounds, perhaps even learned to accept the idiosyncrasies of those around you. However, life often unfolds a new lesson, an ordeal that feels like a tragedy to you. In these moments, you temporarily forget everything you've learned and plunge back into the sensory plane (square 9, Desires), where emotions and desires threaten to engulf you in an unrelenting storm: "I never wanted this! Why me?"

This is a profound lesson that inevitably confronts us in one way or another. To expedite your journey through it and emerge with newfound wisdom, it's imperative that you fully trust the events that unfold and see them as essential lessons tailored for your growth. Don't run from your emotions; instead, observe your resistance to the situation. Are you at peace with the unfolding circumstances?

Ignorance can manifest in various forms, often juxtaposed with the square of human existence. At this level, we understand ourselves as significant beings with a defined purpose and a finite timeline to fulfill it. Unfortunately, these opportunities can be squandered on less consequential pursuits.

If one succumbs to sensory indulgence at this point, the snake may rear its head again. For those coming from square 39, Elimination, the challenge may be to relinquish attachment to someone or something that blocks clear vision and progress. Those coming from square 40, Circulation, are likely to carry unhealed energetic wounds. These wounds may come from toxic relationships that keep them entangled in sensory experiences. Alternatively, the soul may have been on a mission to master the art of making connections, but a painful past event led to an unwarranted withdrawal from such interactions. The soul yearns to connect, and this game reminds you that an intriguing aspect of this endeavor awaits exploration in square 9, Desire. Go and rediscover it!

Exercise: Awareness of Lessons

It's in these trials that the depth of our knowledge is tested. Can we maintain the awareness that our reality is only an illusion? Are we open to perceiving life's events as lessons, as benevolent gifts designed to help rather than punish or be unjust?

ART THAT EVOKES THE SQUARE

- *Samsara* (2011): This documentary takes viewers on a visually stunning journey around the world, highlighting the interconnectedness of all living beings. It encourages viewers to contemplate the karmic cycle of life and rebirth.

The snake only redirects you to square 9, Desires (the sensory plane), if you're still dealing with resentment, fear, pain, or other intense emotions. It's important to address these emotions so that they don't interfere with your pursuit of your life's purpose at higher levels of existence.

45

Suvidya

ACCURATE KNOWLEDGE

To know and not to do is not to know.

GOETHE

Square 45, Suvidya, represents Accurate Knowledge, a powerful source of understanding. Yet, knowledge, when left untouched by experience, remains dormant. It is a state in which an individual relies on this accurate knowledge to stay steadfast on their chosen path.

An individual actively accumulates knowledge, delving into the wisdom of others, making their own discoveries, and endeavoring to apply this newfound wisdom in practical ways. As a result, a treasure trove of knowledge accumulates. At this stage, the player gains the remarkable ability to unify diverse information, to dissect it and see the interconnections, the underlying laws of cause and effect. This knowledge is no longer an encumbrance; it's a seamlessly integrated part of their life. Illusions need not be fabricated, and innovation isn't required.

However, the game sometimes urges the player to seek further learning, to gather information and transform it into knowledge. It's imperative to distinguish between information, the raw data expressed in words, symbols, and diagrams, and knowledge, which embodies the ultimate truth. Knowledge transcends words but must be conveyed through them. In this transition, knowledge may suffer slight distortions, becoming mere information. When you receive information, you must unpack it and transmute it into genuine knowledge. Information often constricts, breeding fear, while knowledge liberates and expands.

Even when armed with true knowledge, the player is not impervious to errors, such as forcing knowledge upon those unseeking of it. In such cases, Violence (square 52) looms just a few moves away. Another pitfall lies in the identification of oneself with knowledge, the misguided belief that "I have the ultimate truth." Periodically, the game may reveal that the player possesses knowledge but, for inexplicable reasons, strays from it, preferring to reside in the realm of illusions. This diversion hampers progress toward Cosmic Consciousness (68) and steers one toward the selfishness of Egocentrism (55).

The journey from the inception of this arrow to its zenith can span many years of a human life. This is logical, for integrating knowledge into one's life demands time, the patience to decipher its practical applications. It is in this process that knowledge is filtered through the sieve of personal experience, gaining genuine value.

Exercise: Information into Knowing

Where are you going to go to learn more, to gather information and turn it into knowing?

ART THAT EVOKES THE SQUARE

- *Journey to the East* by Hermann Hesse: This novella follows the narrator's travels with a mysterious group known as the "League." It delves into the pursuit of wisdom and self-discovery and the challenges in translating knowledge into lived experiences.

Imagine this arrow, symbolizing the embrace of a structured system of knowledge, complete with its limitations, directions, and accepted values. This, in turn, serves as a beacon, saving countless years of one's life by providing a clear direction and a visible road. You are going up to the square of Abandoning Concepts (67), also known as "cosmic good."

LEVEL 6
THE JOURNEY OF THE SELF
Navigating the Cosmic and the Earthly

At this level, the player discovers a profound ability: the power to perceive the world without the veils of societal norms and emotional biases. Here, one embarks on a journey of understanding the intricate workings of the world, shedding extremes and harmonizing internal polarities, such as balancing masculine and feminine aspects, as well as reconciling right and left hemispheric attributes.

It's at this stage that the line between actual reality and the player's imaginary, self-constructed world is clearly drawn. Interaction with actual reality becomes a test encountered only on the seventh level, where the player diligently prepares his body for contact with the Supreme. Failure to relinquish the tendency to create illusions, to nurture the belief in them, and to maintain far-fetched self-images will impede progress and urge the player to descend the serpent of selfishness from square 55 (Egocentrism). At this point, it's crucial to realize that clinging to personal truths is a dangerous pitfall.

46

Viveka
DISCERNMENT

To see things in the seed, that is genius.

LAO TZU

This state embodies a person's ability to fathom the deep meaning, the core essence, of events and phenomena. What seemed complicated in the past now appears remarkably clear and simple. In this state, an individual effortlessly discerns deception and manipulation, and sees the true essence of their surroundings. They can even understand the reasons behind another person's behavior without taking offense.

Being in this square signifies the strength of your inner voice. It implores you to heed its advice. Unlike the previous square, which advocated adherence to a particular system of knowledge, this path is more complicated, but infinitely more compelling. Here, you alone determine what's right or wrong, effective or ineffective; there are no philosophical constructs imposed by others. This journey is marked by independence, not superior or inferior, just different.

Depending on one's level and innate abilities, clairvoyance, clairaudience, and clear knowledge can be activated here. We often imagine these talents to be accompanied by grandiose special effects, but we fail to notice that we already perceive and feel more than before. It's not announced as something extraordinary. These abilities give the player a sense of liberation and weightlessness: "I understand why everything is unfolding the way it is." The individual perceives with the utmost clarity that which brings him closer to happiness.

Mastery of this level involves the ability to see the essence of all things, and to refrain from one-sided judgments and hasty labeling of others. The pitfall of this level is an ardent desire to discover the truth and insist on revealing it in others.

Exercise: Sharing Wisely

Be careful with your extraordinary abilities; remember that not everyone is ready to face the truth about themselves. Use your worldview for personal growth, and share it wisely when others invite you to do so.

ART THAT EVOKES THE SQUARE

- *Awakenings* by Oliver Sacks: The nonfiction book and the subsequent film adaptation tell the story of patients who awaken from decades-long catatonia, highlighting the newfound awareness and discernment they must navigate.

The arrow of discernment leads to the square of Sukh (62), which means "happiness." This arrow represents intuition, the inner voice—and, interestingly, it's the least frequented of all the squares. This suggests that not everyone can easily unlock their inner compass. However, this compass is inherently embedded in every individual's system and provides guidance at life's crossroads. When meeting a new person, it may whisper, "Be cautious" or "this will be a fascinating encounter."

47 Saraswati NEUTRALITY

Nothing is good or bad, but thinking makes it so.

William Shakespeare

Within the realm of existence, there is no absolute concept of good or bad; there's only our response to the unfolding events of life. This square is the point where an individual reaches a state of profound balance and impartiality, forging a harmonious connection between the external world and their inner self. Here, judgment is a foreign concept. Instead, they become a detached observer of both the external world and the workings of their own mind. The need to categorize experiences as good or bad dissolves as they grasp the intricate web of interconnectedness and purpose that surrounds everything.

In this state, the player acquires the remarkable ability to disengage from any identity and flexibly adapt to the demands of any situation. They can activate their yang energy when action is required, and consciously summon their yin energy when serenity and fluidity are in order.

However, a potential pitfall lurks in this plane—the danger of being consumed by neutrality, drifting into an excessive state of detachment, and losing interest in life's pursuits. Questions arise: Why go anywhere? Why do anything? These are dangerous thoughts. In the great game of life, one must always ask, "Why live?" For as long as one is alive, there's a purpose, a journey to be undertaken. To avoid the clutches of neutrality, it's crucial to maintain an insatiable curiosity about life's mysteries and remain open to the inexhaustible wonders that await.

Exercise: Remaining Open to Life

To avoid being numbed by neutrality, ask yourself, "What will be interesting next?"

ART THAT EVOKES THE SQUARE

- *Equilibrium* (2002): In this dystopian sci-fi film, society seeks to eliminate emotions to achieve peace and neutrality, but the protagonist discovers the importance of experiencing positive and negative feelings.
- *The Giver* (2014): Directed by Phillip Noyce, this film is based on Lois Lowry's award-winning novel. Set in a society that suppresses emotions and memories to maintain order, the story follows Jonas, who is chosen to receive humanity's memories from The Giver. As Jonas discovers love, pain, and individuality, he begins to question the oppressive control of his world.

48

Yamuna
SOLAR PLANE

Do not go where the path may lead, go instead where there is no path and leave a trail.

RALPH WALDO EMERSON

This square, the Solar Plane, represents the energy of sheer determination, an unwavering force directed toward a specific outcome. When this solar energy is out of balance, flowing weakly, it becomes a challenge for an individual to manifest their desires, take active steps, and shape their life as a creator. Conversely, when this energy is excessive and out of balance, the individual tends to act with excessive aggression, brashness, and arrogance. They become independent and may look down on those they perceive as weaker. Their decisions are seen as the only correct ones, and they struggle to respect the opinions of others, bordering on obsession. This unrestrained wave of energy is in danger of consuming everything in its path, including the player's well-being.

Solar energy primarily affects the right side of the body and is typically associated with masculine traits. However, it's important to note that both lunar and solar energies are present in all of us, regardless of gender. Solar energy is central to creative endeavors and purposeful action. When this solar energy is dominant in one's life, it's the time to shine and contribute to society. It's a phase marked by outward focus, a period of activity, and the realization of carefully crafted plans.

During this phase, the game sends a clear message to the player: "Move forward, take action, make progress!" The player is encouraged to channel their solar energy to achieve tangible results, signaling readiness for new triumphs and accomplishments.

Exercise: Expression of Your Solar Energy

1. Consider how your solar energy expresses itself. Do you find it effortless to make decisions? Can you transform ideas into tangible reality, or do they linger in the realm of the abstract?
2. When you do bring an idea to life, do you maintain a healthy perspective on your goals? Can you avoid overwhelming yourself and others with excessive pressure? Remember, concentrating all the energy of the sun onto a single point can result in burning everything in its path.

ART THAT EVOKES THE SQUARE

- *The Art of Racing in the Rain* by Garth Stein: This novel explores the world through the eyes of a dog named Enzo, emphasizing the determination and commitment of its owner, a race car driver.
- *Open Your Eyes* (1997): This Spanish film explores the protagonist's determination to reconstruct his life after a disfiguring accident, delving into themes of determination and transformation.

49
Ganga
MOON PLANE

The quieter you become, the more you can hear.

Ram Dass

Ganga, a celestial river and the embodiment of abundant life and fertility, represents the Lunar Plane where the essence of feminine and yin energy converge. This square focuses on the magnetic force of attraction, and lunar actions prioritize the journey rather than the final destination. When lunar energy is deficient, the player may struggle to maintain gentleness and smoothness in their actions, potentially leading to an overflow of solar energy, undue aggression, and destructive behavior.

Lunar energy is centered on acceptance. In cases of excessive lunar energy, the player may collect indiscriminately, even accumulating what is unnecessary in body and mind. This phase provides an opportunity for the player to harmonize their lunar energy, allowing them to attract what's essential and select the most valuable elements.

In contrast to solar energy, the lunar period encourages contemplation and introspection, illuminating the deepest recesses of the soul in search of answers. It's a time of silence, respite, and tranquility. Energy accumulates, recuperation takes place, and rejuvenation occurs. In this moment, existence is only for oneself, shielded from the demands of the world.

Exercise: Your Inner Landscape

Take your time to be with you; contemplate what's going on in your inner landscape. What do you want to seed? What is happening within you during this time, and where is your inner light leading you?

ART THAT EVOKES THE SQUARE

- *Spring, Summer, Fall, Winter . . . and Spring* (2003): This South Korean film explores the life of a Buddhist monk and his introspective journey through the changing seasons.

50 Tapa Loka AUSTERITY

Simplicity is the ultimate sophistication.

LEONARDO DA VINCI

A sanctuary for profound self-reflection and solitude, Tapa Loka (square 50) represents the concentrated strength of one's conscience. Austerity embraces the virtues of self-discipline, detachment, and the unwavering fulfillment of vows. When the player acts from the depths of their heart, they realize that the pursuit of material possessions and relationships is not the key to happiness. What truly ignites their joy is the authentic expression of their soul and the resounding call of their heart.

Soul desires reign supreme at the top of the pyramid—everything else takes a back seat. To traverse the path to fulfill these soul desires, one must be willing to give up all other distractions. This requires immense willpower, as a person may have numerous talents and longings for various endeavors. However, even pursuits that bring solace to the soul must be set aside in order to focus on what is most important.

To walk the path of asceticism, the player must recognize and trust the divine essence within. This trust unlocks the vision and hearing often referred to as the "third eye." To unlock it, one must shed unnecessary layers around and within, purifying the mind. In truth, you already see and hear everything, but the relentless barrage of thoughts, fears, and emotions obscures this awareness. Once the player lets go of worries, attachments, and the fear of scarcity, they move forward with ease.

The main pitfall on this level is the misinterpretation of asceticism. Rushing to "enlightenment" by cutting all ties, neglecting one's own health, and living a life of hardship or self-torment does not lead to purification or a higher vibrational state. Such actions are rooted in desire and greed. Furthermore, taking care of one's body is an essential and fundamental lesson. Neglecting this task may necessitate a return to this point. An indicator that one has gone too far into austerity is advancement to square 52, Violence, which often occurs when a person imposes their ascetic practices on others.

Exercise: Commitment to Your Soul's Path

The work of this square may involve embarking on a new and unfamiliar journey that brings you closer to your inner self. Even if you encounter resistance at first, once you take the first step, you may find an unstoppable force propelling you forward. What obstacle do you need to overcome right now? What action demands your attention? Conquering means committing to something that isn't effortless, yet you understand it to be the right path from the perspective of your soul.

ART THAT EVOKES THE SQUARE

- *The Razor's Edge* (1984): Based on W. Somerset Maugham's novel, the film centers on a man's pursuit of meaning and enlightenment through asceticism and self-discovery.
- *Seven Years in Tibet* (1997): Inspired by the true story of Heinrich Harrer's relationship with the 14th Dalai Lama, the film delves into themes of purpose, friendship, and spirituality.

51 Prithvi THE EARTH

> *Life is a game, play it. Life is a challenge, meet it. Life is an adventure, dare it.*
>
> MOTHER TERESA

Earth serves as a vast playground, offering a multitude of opportunities for human interaction and expression. It presents an infinite canvas for play, more diverse and abundant than at any time in human history. Our presence here is indeed a remarkable gift, and it is imperative that we treat this wondrous place with the utmost respect, for it offers us an extraordinary life experience.

The Earth resiliently endures all trials and tribulations, offering a lasting embrace to all that unfolds upon its surface. She maintains her affection for her inhabitants, regardless of the different paths they take. Furthermore, Earth possesses the wisdom to recognize and bestow her blessings upon those who revere the planet and participate harmoniously in this celestial game.

Here on Earth, we are discovering a realm where we can boldly express our individuality while respecting the autonomy of our fellow inhabitants and the shared space in which we coexist. This terrestrial sphere serves as a sanctuary where we become aware of our inherent worth while recognizing our humble place in the vast tapestry of existence. This humility, a priceless quality, guides us toward material success and empowers us to realize our limitless potential. In this space, we confront the paradox of being both significant and diminutive.

Once we realize that our purpose here is to participate in this grand game, the fear of life dissolves. Players are willing to reveal their true selves, adapt, explore different roles, and enjoy the game to the fullest. Is the Earth expressing gratitude for our presence? Its only request is that we engage in the game and enjoy our unique roles. The greatest misstep on Earth is to reside without actively participating in the games we've designed. If a player is afraid to embody the human experience on Earth, if they find this world threatening or ominous, they risk descending to Egocentrism (55) where they withdraw from the world and seek refuge in the self-constructed realm of illusion.

Exercise: Your Earthly Self

How do you unleash your inner self? If you've arrived back to The Earth (51) via the serpent of Unconsciousness (72), what facets of your character have yet to be revealed during your earthly sojourn?

ART THAT EVOKES THE SQUARE

- *The Hidden Life of Trees* by Peter Wohlleben: This book uncovers the interconnected and often hidden relationships among trees and their environment, offering a unique perspective on Earth's hidden wonders.
- *The Unexpected Truth About Animals* by Lucy Cooke: This book explores the often surprising and interconnected relationships between various animal species and their role in the ecosystem. It sheds light on the hidden and unexpected behaviors of animals, revealing the intricacies of life on Earth in a captivating way.

52
Himsa Loka
VIOLENCE

Violence is the last refuge of the incompetent.

Isaac Asimov

The transition to this realm is a formidable challenge that tests the depth of human understanding achieved in the previous stages. It tests whether one truly embraces others, respects their opinions and desires, or whether gaps in learning remain. Armed with a vast array of knowledge and accomplishments, humans often tend to offer unsolicited guidance from a well-intentioned perspective, believing they know what's best.

However, if a person disregards the interests of others, advances without considering their perspectives, imposes their will, and believes their viewpoint is the only correct one, they find themselves descending to the realm of Naraka Loka, Purgatory (square 35). Violence can lurk under the guise of good intentions: "I know exactly what to do! I'll help you; you can't do it alone!" Imposing one's knowledge and experience can be a form of violence. At the lowest level, people may have resorted to violence out of fear, self-defense, or to assert their beliefs. Here, the player demonstrates an unwavering belief that they are helping others by forcing them to conform to their own experiences, essentially depriving them of their right to follow their own unique paths. This is not genuine concern; it lacks love.

In particular, Carl Rogers, a prominent humanistic psychologist, argued that imposing oneself on others, even with benevolent intentions, can manifest as a form of violence.[1] Rogers contended that when an individual dismisses or overrides another's feelings and desires, it undermines empathy and understanding, potentially leading to conflict masked as goodwill. In Greek mythology, the story of Prometheus illustrates this concept. Prometheus stole fire from the gods to give to humanity, a seemingly benevolent act. However, this act of generosity was perceived as a challenge to divine authority and resulted in severe retribution from the gods. This narrative underscores how even acts of altruism can be construed as violent when they challenge the established order.

Yet violence is not only directed at others; it is often self-inflicted. People often become entangled in obligations and spend most of their days fulfilling them, neglecting the desires of their souls and forcing themselves into activities for which they have no real inclination. This self-imposed compulsion may manifest itself in statements such as "I forced myself to exercise in spite of physical discomfort," or "I forced myself to befriend my neighbor in spite of inner resistance." Conversely, individuals may be so preoccupied with their duties that they ignore their inner impulses. When their soul yearns for something, they invent a multitude of excuses for why it can't occur, such as "I can't afford it," or "They won't understand me," or "How will I make it happen?"

Another form of violence occurs when individuals become overly and rigidly attached to the principles of nonviolence. Their actions or inactions may become inappropriate and even dangerous because they allow their own boundaries to be overstepped, threatening their integrity and well-being. For example, the commitment to do no harm to living beings may lead one to refrain from defending oneself against an attacker or an aggressive animal.

Violence stems from beliefs, misunderstandings, and faulty programming. One must not only recognize where and how violence is committed but also correct their actions. They can learn from the past, but must not lose sight of the present, lest they fall back into that realm.

Exercise: How Does Violence Manifest in Your Life?

1. Consider how violence manifests in your life. Take some time to record these expressions.
2. Using the skills you have gained thus far, analyze what you have written. How can you proceed so that you don't return to this square again?

ART THAT EVOKES THE SQUARE

- *Ordinary People* (1980): This film that explores the aftermath of a family tragedy and the emotional violence that can fester within.

You must embark on a journey of purification, descending into the square of Purgatory (35), to get rid of violence. This is not punitive, but a profound cleansing process. If you evade responsibility for your actions, your passage through Purgatory will be arduous, and you may be in danger of descending even further.

53

Jala Loka

LIQUID PLANE

Nothing is softer or more flexible than water, yet nothing can resist it.

Lao Tzu

Life unfolds naturally, following a continuous stream of events. One event leads to another, and change is constant. This ceaseless movement is the essence of life itself.

The Liquid Plane delves into the concept of flow and reflects the qualities of water. Water has the ability to cool, calm emotional turmoil, cleanse, and nourish. When we find ourselves in this space, it serves as a reminder to cultivate the inherent qualities of water within ourselves—fluidity, flexibility, softness, movement, and trust. Where do we need to be more adaptable? In what situations should we surrender to the flow, trust, and refrain from fixating on outcomes or individuals? Things don't always go as planned, not because the Universe is working against us, but because it recognizes the most beneficial path for us, one that may be unpredictable and unexpected.

When we internalize the qualities of water, we become serene, capable of assuming any form, much like water that takes on the shape of its container. Rigid boundaries dissolve and we become adaptable to situation and intention, rendering ourselves unmanageable.

Water embodies constant transformation, capable of becoming steam or ice. It never stagnates, except in stagnant waters that eventually become foul. For water to remain pure and alive, it requires movement. Water particles in the clouds today become rain tomorrow, nourish the Earth on Monday, and are part of the apple we enjoy for breakfast on Wednesday. As water cycles through these stages, it accumulates and imparts a wealth of information. Water has this ability to offer and absorb information because of its fluidity. This facet of water teaches us not to hoard energy, be it money, emotions, or knowledge. Do we share our knowledge or do we feel unprepared to share it? Do we hoard money, fearing its loss, or are we reluctant to spend it? Money, like water, thrives on circulation and resists stagnation in a single bank account.

Water is also characterized by acceptance and dissolution. Anything thrown into water will eventually settle to the bottom. Water dissolves various substances, seemingly making them disappear while changing its own properties. Sometimes the game leads us to this place to melt the ice within us, to soften our rough and cold edges. At other times, it urges us to calm the boiling waters within. It's important to recognize that water can be destructive, stirring up storms or submerging us. In such cases, we need to calm the turbulence within us.

When there is an excess of water in a person, it scatters. It loses its ability to take a definite form or to act purposefully; it becomes completely subservient to its surroundings and becomes excessively passive.

Exercise: Flow Like Water

How does water manifest in you? Are you open to shedding tears? How do your emotions flow? How adaptable are you?

ART THAT EVOKES THE SQUARE

- *The Persistence of Memory* by Salvador Dalí: This painting is an iconic example of surrealism, an artistic movement that often explores the transformation and illusory nature of time. The melting clocks in the painting symbolize the constant flux of time and reality (1931, oil on canvas, Museum of Modern Art, New York).

54 Bhakti DEVOTION

With every breath, I plant the seeds of devotion
I am a farmer of the heart.

RUMI

Bhakti is not submission to a deity. It is falling in love with the Mystery. To live in God means to see the manifestation of the Divine within oneself, to recognize the talents and abilities given by the Divine, and to act in accordance with them. Essentially, when you use your talents and abilities as intended, you are in harmony, ready to transcend illusion, and approaching the end of this cosmic game.

In a state of spiritual surrender, the player perceives the Divine in all things. Every person encountered on the journey, regardless of their actions or behavior, is seen as a manifestation of the Divine. Even in moments of violence, anger, or error, the player recognizes it as the play of the Divine within people.

This is the only arrow that leads you directly to Cosmic Consciousness. But it is not completion. It is arrival. This is where the player understands that there is only love and everything else is just an illusion. This realization transcends the realm of the mind; it pervades the entire being. On the mental plane, it manifests as a profound love for the Divine, filling the player with joy and gratitude for the intricacies of this game called life. The player recognizes the wise design of existence and feels incredibly fortunate to be a part of it.

There is no exercise or work of art that can depict this state, as it transcends verbalization and materialization; it is a pure, experiential phenomenon.

You are going directly to the square of Cosmic Consciousness (68). You have finished the game.

LEVEL 7
DANCING BETWEEN LIGHT AND DARKNESS

Upon ascending to the seventh level of personal development, the player shatters the illusion of duality. At this sublime stage, the vibrations are so elevated that an individual undergoes a profound transformation in their perception of themselves and others. The incessant restlessness dissipates, replaced by a detached observation of oneself from an external perspective, recognizing one's place as part of a vast and interconnected world. It's here that one begins to gather answers to one's questions from a multitude of sources, seemingly drawn from the cosmos itself. In this realm, the player awakens to their rightful claim to understanding their existence within a reality they've actively shaped through a lifetime of thought and action.

With each upward step, the player encounters increasingly complex and dangerous challenges, made apparent by the longer and more treacherous snakes that inhabit this realm of the game. As the player's level escalates, so does the burden of responsibility. Whereas in the lower levels, responsibility was primarily for actions and later expanded to include words, at this level it even includes thoughts and emotions.

If a player remains too attached to the material world, they'll find it difficult to maintain their footing. It's only when one learns the art of detachment, releasing one's grip on worldly attachments and embracing the true nature of reality, that one can ascend without stumbling.

55

Ahamkara
EGOCENTRISM

The more you make this world about you, the more miserable you will be.

MATT CHANDLER

Egocentrism is a frequently visited snake. It's interesting that the Bhakti and Ahamkara squares are next to each other. Where Bhakti speaks to the divine through presence and trust, Ahamkara drowns in its own voice. One becomes trapped inside their own echo, convinced of their authority over reality.

Self-centeredness isn't just about prioritizing one's own needs and desires; it's a state in which a person becomes disconnected from the world, the Universe, and other people. This disconnection leads to a sharp descent into the Anger square (3). In this state, it may seem that no one understands them, the Universe doesn't care, and they are isolated with no one to help them. The world is suddenly perceived as hostile, and anger arises toward the world that has seemingly turned its back on them.

In reality, the person has isolated themselves from the outside world by putting up a metaphorical wall. It's not the world that has become hostile; it's their internal fears that create aggression toward the outside world.

In early life, egocentrism is natural—the child's psyche hasn't yet grown into empathy. But in adulthood, when the soul should have widened its view, Ahamkara lingers as the scar of unmet needs. The ego and self-awareness are necessary for existence and personal identity; they can become limiting when they begin to confine us, leading to the emergence of self-centeredness. *Aham* means "I" and *kara* means "form"—it means the form that shapes and can also limit the self. Limiting beliefs about oneself are likely to contribute to this.

In a state of self-centeredness, you effectively exclude God from your worldview. You find yourself in perpetual disagreement with God's decisions, constantly trying to correct what you perceive as unfair situations. You may argue that certain events shouldn't have happened, or that you or others don't deserve such experiences. This state keeps you in a perpetual argument with God, as you strive to demonstrate that you know better and can handle things more competently. As a result, you exert excessive control.

This burden of playing God becomes increasingly heavy, causing your shoulders to ache, perhaps even metaphorically bleeding. However, it's important to realize that the invitation to set this burden down is always near. There is mercy in remembering you are not in charge of the stars—that your place is not to govern, but to co-create.

Exercise: An Inventory of Egocentrism

List behaviors, situations, or thought patterns that demonstrate egocentrism.

ART THAT EVOKES THE SQUARE

- *Notes from Underground* by Fyodor Dostoevsky: This novel explores the inner thoughts and actions of a highly egocentric narrator.

You are going to the square of Anger (3). To escape the pit of self-centeredness, players must first take responsibility for their situation. They must pause and find solid ground, acknowledge their imperfections, and realize that the Universe cares for and loves each of us. The ideal square following such a fall is Compassion (17), indicating that the person has reconnected to and is in harmony with the world. Subsequent moves will reveal the best way to overcome self-centeredness and embrace the newfound emotions and connections.

56
Omkara
DIVINE SOUND

The power of sound creates the illusion of the invisible.

Claude Debussy

Everything is vibration. According to the teaching of the vibrational and wave structure of the world, there are no solid bodies, no time, no space; everything is simply a manifestation of energy in vibration. Omkara is both a mantra and a prayer, and is believed to help focus on the essential. It sets the energetic channels in motion, releasing blockages and tensions, allowing you to release your true voice.

Each person arrives on Earth with their unique set of vibrations, much like a beautiful musical instrument. Humanity collectively creates a beautiful divine symphony that harmonizes with other beings, objects, and phenomena. However, under the influence of stress, negative emotions, and aggressive actions, our strings can become tense, frayed, or loose. How would such an instrument sound? It would be out of tune, disrupting the harmony of the great orchestra. When the vibrations are out of balance, discomfort and suffering arise, and the body may begin to hurt.

Omkara encourages us to express ourselves through sound, to let our souls resonate. In this square the player can fine-tune their vibrations and rediscover their true sound on Earth. This square addresses all aspects of the player's relationship with sound. For example, it may be time to assert oneself and speak loudly to be heard, or conversely, to find a softer and quieter tone.

The Chinese philosopher Confucius emphasized the importance of harmony in society and life, and the role of music in promoting balance and cohesion. This suggests that sound affects not only the individual but also the way people interact in society, enriching our understanding of vibration as a tool for social harmony.

Exercise: Expressing Your Will

Can you effectively express your will with your voice? Do you know how to communicate to be heard in the right way, at the right time, and with the right intensity? Do you know when to be silent?

ART THAT EVOKES THE SQUARE

- *Music for 18 Musicians* by Steve Reich: This album is a minimalist composition that uses repetitive patterns and phase shifting to create a mesmerizing sonic experience, highlighting the transformative power of sound and rhythm (ECM Records, 1978).
- *The Sound of a Wild Snail Eating* by Elisabeth Tova Bailey: This memoir explores the author's deep connection with a snail and the vibrations and sounds of nature, revealing the harmony in seemingly small and insignificant moments.

57

Vayu Loka

AIR PLANE

> *As you breathe in, cherish yourself. As you breathe out, cherish all beings.*
>
> DALAI LAMA

In the realm of the Liquid Plane (square 53), a person becomes capable of assuming different forms, but here in the Air Plane, the need for a specific form disappears. High vibrations make an individual as light as air itself, allowing everything to flow through them without altering their essence.

Air is closely associated with lightness, and in this state one experiences an unburdened freedom, without the weight of constant control or obsessive worry about whether things are working as planned. This square reminds us that intuition is not a mystical gift, but a natural byproduct of attunement. It is important not to distort the perception of events with fear and doubt, but rather understanding what is happening and why.

It's not a matter of persistently knocking on a closed door, insisting on your own way, but of attentively listening to the messages that the space around you is conveying. Air imparts the wisdom of intuitive awareness and a sensitive perception of the situation: knowing when to slow down or, conversely, to accelerate based on the dynamics of the space. This ability to sense space transforms the quality of one's daily life, guiding one to take precise actions that are consistently timely and effective.

Understanding how to merge with the energy of the surrounding space, learning to follow its lead, and being guided by it are key aspects. The space already knows what actions will lead where and how best to express oneself in each moment. At such an elevated vibrational level, a person becomes the embodiment of pure flow, much like the breath itself, and experiences a profound sense of liberation.

However, operating at these high vibrational frequencies carries the risk of dissolution. The sensations of lightness and weightlessness can be so intoxicating that an individual may lose sight of their purpose in the grand game and disregard the needs of their own body. They may become scattered, lose concentration, and struggle to focus on anything of significance. The surrounding world may seem to lose its meaning. In Greek mythology, we can draw a parallel with the story of Icarus, who flew too close to the sun with wings made of wax and feathers. As he approached the sun, the wings melted and he fell into the sea. Icarus symbolizes the idea that excessive soaring without caution can lead to euphoria and detachment from reality, similar to the potential of dissolving into the realm of air due to exceptionally high vibrations. Air, then, is both gift and test. It brings inspiration, but demands presence. It teaches movement, but requires grounding.

Exercise: Concentration Practice

Begin your concentration practice with a five-minute *Om* mantra chant. Initially, you can use a YouTube video featuring a person chanting the *Om* mantra, following along with them. As you progress, consider gradually extending the duration of your practice.

ART THAT EVOKES THE SQUARE

- *Music for Airports* by Brian Eno: This ambient music album creates a sense of spaciousness and weightlessness, perfect for evoking the qualities of air (Editions EG, 1978).
- *Wings of Desire* (1987): This poetic German film directed by Wim Wenders explores the lives of angels who observe human existence, touching on the idea of detachment and awareness.

58

Loka Roff Tile

LIGHT PLANE

> *All the darkness in the world cannot extinguish the light of a single candle.*
>
> Francis of Assisi

A joyful person is often described as having bright, shining eyes, which is more than just a figurative expression. Their eyes actually radiate light. Children and those with heightened sensitivities can perceive this radiant quality, seeing people in a luminous state as emitting a stronger, brighter light. Søren Kierkegaard emphasized the importance of living an authentic and passionate life,[1] fully engaging with existence and unearthing the inner light. Those who live authentic and passionate lives can indeed radiate a distinctive luminosity because of their authenticity and commitment to their core values and aspirations.

When a person's vibrations rise to such elevated levels, they begin to radiate light. Even subconsciously, those around them take notice. When they enter a room, it's as if they fill it with their radiance. People are naturally drawn to them, eager to bask in their luminous presence. The light emanating from this person dispels the darkness. Those with lower vibrations or destructive tendencies instinctively stay away. In their presence, everything seems straightforward and clear, much like being in the presence of Athena, the goddess of wisdom and strategy in Greek mythology. Athena is often depicted with a radiant crown of light emanating from her forehead, symbolizing intelligence and clarity of thought. It may be related to the idea that where this radiance shines, everything becomes uncomplicated and clear.

In this state, a person attracts appropriate events and circumstances. When they ask a question, information flows to them from various sources. Occasionally, a person who enters the Light Plane will become anxious about their state. They may not understand why animals and strangers are drawn to them while others try to avoid them. Furthermore, it's possible that a player who attracts the people they need with their radiance may not even realize it, thus missing the gifts that are sent to them in response to their inner desires.

Exercise: Without Intentionality

This state cannot be reached intentionally, and when a person enters it, they may not even be aware of it. If a person becomes aware of this state and attaches too much importance to it, they might go astray. That's why there's no practice to intentionally achieve this state.

ART THAT EVOKES THE SQUARE

- *The Light Inside* by James Turrell: Turrell's light installations explore the perceptual experience of light and space, creating an environment of inner radiance (1999, Museum of Fine Arts, Houston, Texas).
- *The Prophet* by Kahlil Gibran: This book of poetic essays touches upon various aspects of life and spirituality, including the radiance of the soul.

59
Satya Loka
THE TRUTH

Life can only be understood backwards; but it must be lived forwards.

SØREN KIERKEGAARD

The seventh chakra proclaims the right to knowledge, and this square, Satya Loka or The Truth, is where that right is exercised. This concept can be likened to Plato's allegory of the cave, where people chained in a cave perceive the shadows on the wall as their only reality. However, when one of them breaks free and sees the sunlight outside, they experience a profound revelation of true reality. This allegory highlights how our perception of truth can drastically change when confronted with new perspectives, leading to the discovery of a deeper reality.

In this state, as the player remembers themselves as an individual yet in unity with all, true reality is revealed. The player becomes fulfilled and ceases to search for the meaning of life, realizing that the meaning lies within themselves. They understand that the essence of life lies in living a human existence.

On the plane of Truth, the player lets go of the idea of living an extraordinary life or becoming superhuman. Instead, they embrace simplicity and understand that they are both the source and the reason for the reflections in their reality. Everyone has a unique reality. The key is not to distance oneself from others, as this can lead to feelings of deep isolation and an inability to share one's reality with others. To avoid this, one should strive to take an interest in how others perceive and create their own realities.

The challenge in the realm of reality is the lack of alignment with it. The player may finally perceive reality as it is but find it unpleasant or intimidating. The next move will reveal how the player overcomes this lesson. If they are unwilling to accept reality and pass judgment on it, they may encounter Negativity (square 61). If reality frightens them and they continue to cling to their illusions, they may descend to Tamas (Darkness, square 63) and then to Maya (Illusion, square 2).

Exercise: Connect to a Different Perspective

In the coming days, make an effort to connect with someone who holds a perspective radically different from your own, and try to immerse yourself in their state of mind and worldview. This task may be challenging, but the more often you practice it, the stronger and more attuned your energy channel will become.

ART THAT EVOKES THE SQUARE

- *Waking Life* (2001): Directed by Richard Linklater, this animated film delves into philosophical and existential discussions, touching on the nature of reality and truth.

60

Subudhi

POSITIVITY

You must be the change you wish to see in the world.

MAHATMA GANDHI

Subudhi, the state of pure mind, represents a profound change in one's approach to life. It's not about positive thinking, which can sometimes lead to denial or suppression of true emotions. In square 60, Subudhi, the player transcends the duality of good and evil and accepts events as experiences to be learned from.

This state can be compared to the humanistic psychology approach of Carl Rogers, who advocated empathy and unconditional acceptance of one's experiences and emotions.[2] Similarly, Subudhi encourages unconditional acceptance of one's reality without labeling it as good or bad.

It's important to understand, however, that this acceptance does not lead to passivity or inaction. Instead, the individual learns to act in harmony with the situation at hand, conserving energy that would otherwise be spent evaluating and categorizing events. This allows for a more balanced response to life's joys, sorrows, and complexities.

In this state, one experiences quiet joy and deep sadness without becoming overly absorbed in analyzing these emotions. The focus remains on living, gaining valuable experience, and progressing toward personal goals.

Subudhi teaches us that every shade of emotion contributes to our holistic experience and understanding of life.

Exercise: Create Without Judgment

Engage in creative and contemplative practices—such as art, poetry, or music—and express your thoughts and emotions through these arts without imposing judgment. Let your creativity flow without trying to categorize your work as "good" or "bad."

Remember that developing the trait of subudhi is a gradual process, and you may encounter challenges along the way. Be patient with yourself, and continue practicing self-acceptance and nonjudgment.

ART THAT EVOKES THE SQUARE

- *The Book of Disquiet* by Fernando Pessoa: This philosophical and introspective work delves into the complex inner world of its main character, emphasizing contemplation and acceptance.

61

Durbudhi
NEGATIVITY

You are not a drop in the ocean. You are the entire ocean in a drop.

Attributed to Rumi

In a state of positivity, an individual learns to trust the unfolding of events and sees purpose in everything that happens. As a result, they move through life without fear. In contrast, in a state of negative intellect, a player loses faith and begins to doubt. This descent into negativity often occurs when one succumbs to the temptation to return to dualistic thinking: "This is wrong," "It should be different," "They are wrong." The individual begins to judge the course of events, resists them, and becomes emotionally charged. Resistance to reality ultimately leads to a fall into insignificance.

In this state, the individual devalues their entire journey, their knowledge, and even reality itself. Essentially, they lose faith in themselves and in the divine essence within. They begin to feel small, to believe that their efforts are in vain, and that their knowledge has no meaning. Engaging in a struggle against reality drains their energy and leaves them feeling powerless.

Exercise: Avoid Judgment

During this phase, much attention is paid to the values of others. Are you judging someone? Do you compare yourself to others? Do you think that someone around you is thinking wrongly? These thoughts are traps. Each person acts according to their unique path. This is part of the universal design, regardless of whether the player feels it is right or wrong.

ART THAT EVOKES THE SQUARE

- *The Tunnel* by Ernesto Sabato: This novel explores themes of alienation and existential crisis, where the protagonist becomes engulfed in self-doubt and negativity.
- *Blindness* by José Saramago: This novel explores a sudden epidemic of blindness and its effects on society, delving into the darker aspects of human nature.

You venture into the Nullity square (13) to relearn the art of refraining from comparisons and judgments, returning once more to the mindset of a student.

62
Sukh
HAPPINESS

Joy is not in things; it is in us.

Richard Wagner

Sukh means "lightness," "comfort," and "joy." It's the daily, fleeting happiness that is often based on external reasons: a loved one, a purchase, a sunny day, or some other cause for joy. On this level, the player finds a reason to be happy. However, it's important to remember that emotions that depend on external conditions can be temporary. The source of happiness can disappear at any time. If the player can let go, knowing that another reason for happiness will come along, they will discern the lesson of this square and reach a state of complete harmony and balance.

In this positive mental state, the player leaves behind all their fears, suffering, resentment, and anger. The nearness of the fulfillment of their desires fills them with joyful anticipation. If the player rolls a six during this phase, he can ascend to Cosmic Consciousness and complete the game.

The happiness experienced in this state is so delightful that the player may wish to prolong it. However, if the player becomes too dependent on the cause of their happiness, they may fall into a trap, fearing the loss of this fragile state of joy. However, true and lasting happiness doesn't depend on getting what you want. Understanding this concept empowers the player and frees them from the consuming desire for external fulfillment.

The state described here represents the first level of happiness, and there is a higher form of happiness to be experienced that doesn't diminish personal freedom. When the player understands that happiness doesn't depend solely on the fulfillment of desires, they become incredibly powerful, and the passion for desire will no longer consume them. Other states of joy often depend on circumstances and external factors, whereas this deeper happiness comes from within.

Exercise: The Source of Happiness

What is the source of your happiness? Does it stem from external factors, or do you naturally emanate happiness from your very being?

ART THAT EVOKES THE SQUARE

- *The Red Balloon* (1956): This short film directed by Albert Lamorisse tells the story of a young boy who discovers joy in an unexpected friendship with a red balloon.

63
Tamas
DARKNESS

The difference between passion and obsession is that between a divine spark and a flame that incinerates.

GABOR MATÉ

The longest snake of the game takes the player from this square, Tamas (Darkness), into the square of Maya (Illusion), a place where they may not be fully prepared to advance to the eighth level. Sometimes a player will have ascended so far that they mistakenly believe they've completed all their lessons and think they don't need to grow any further. Alternatively, a player who's very close to achieving their desires may become obsessed with their goal and place undue importance on achieving it. In either case, the individual falls into the trap of illusion, which can lead to despair and thoughts like, "Why do I have to start all over again?" That's when the temptation to give up arises.

But it's important to examine this snake closely, because it's the same uroboros that bites its own tail. Uroboros symbolizes the cycle of death and rebirth, offering the opportunity to be reborn and encounter all the lessons again, but this time armed with new knowledge. It provides a fresh perspective on past situations, allowing one to reexperience what didn't work before and emerge enriched.

In most cases, the player will progress quickly, unless despair and loss of faith slow them down, causing them to stay in the same place, going in circles.

This concept serves as a reminder of the importance of staying aware of our personal growth and not falling into inertia. Life is filled with cycles of learning and rebirth, much like the Hindu philosophy of reincarnation and rebirth. These ideas intertwine to enrich our understanding of inertia and the need to learn from our experiences in order to progress on our spiritual journey.

Exercise: Contemplate What Brought You Here

Which thoughts, motivations, or concepts guided you to this point? In what ways did they deviate from your expectations? Where did you encounter stumbling blocks? Did your initial motive come from a place of purity, or did you find yourself once again yearning for external validation, placing too much emphasis on financial outcomes, or compromising for less than you deserve?

Occasionally, our pursuits falter because they aren't aligned with our surroundings. It may seem like the world doesn't support us, causing us to lower our expectations even further, but perhaps we should have aimed higher.

ART THAT EVOKES THE SQUARE

- *Lord of the Flies* by William Golding: This novel explores the descent of a group of young boys into savagery and chaos when they are stranded on a deserted island, making grave mistakes along the way.

Darkness leads you to the square of Illusion (2).

LEVEL 8

THE HIGHER SELF

Connecting with the Divine

At this zenith, the player attains the highest level imaginable within the earthly realm and establishes a connection with the Guardians of the World. At this point, the individual receives guidance and support from the higher powers or their own higher self. While not everything at this level can be grasped through rational understanding, much unfolds at the level of sensation and emotion that defies verbal articulation. However, such limitations are insignificant. What really matters is the soul's internalization of these messages.

64
Prakriti Loka
PHENOMENAL PLANE

My wish is to stay always like this, living quietly in a corner of nature.

CLAUDE MONET

Prakriti, the initial creation, serves as the fundamental cause of the tangible world. It is at this stage that a profound comprehension of our planet's existence becomes attainable, enabling us to engage with the Earth and its spirit. Arriving at this square serves as a reminder of the significance of momentarily setting aside our pressing duties and simply immersing ourselves in nature. Such moments provide a keen sense of being present in the here and now. When you retreat to solitary sojourns by the riverside, amid mountains, in the forest, or by the sea, you open the door to receive messages from your spirit guides and helpers.

In this phase, it's essential to connect with the feminine aspect of your identity to truly sense the Earth. When you attune yourself to her, you become an extension of the Earth, and in return, she offers her resources to support you.

We're introduced to a world from the moment of birth, a world that our minds comprehend and our senses perceive as reality. Yet, as we progress through the seven levels of the game, we come to realize that the reality we've known is nothing more than a game. Living in cities, we inhabit concrete reflections of human ideas. And in the postmodern era, we no longer live in the original, but in copies of a copy that distance us from the source.

In the Phenomenal Plane, everything exists and all possibilities abound—it's a realm of ideas and creativity. At this stage, our divine essence has conceptualized a game, determining the nature of our existence, the experiences we will encounter, the people we will meet, and the paths we will traverse. When one reaches this level, they are prepared to witness how the Universe and its Spirit have conceived and executed the plan to facilitate the necessary experiences for the player. Here, the player willingly embraces their lessons, for they remember that they once chose them. Occasionally, at this stage and in particular states, the player may realize they can relinquish certain lessons. They gain the capacity to make their own choices, marking a pivotal moment: Having surmounted numerous trials, they can opt for different lessons and revisit the previous ones in a future life. Your journey continues, and you are now equipped to make your own decisions.

This square invites a return—not only to the forest, the river, the sea—but to the deeper memory of our divine essence. It serves as a reminder that life is a game in which we select the lessons we wish to learn.

Exercise: Pause and Reflect

This square offers an opportunity to pause and reflect. Ask yourself, "Where am I headed? Have I neglected something crucial? Have I overlooked something?"

ART THAT EVOKES THE SQUARE

- *The Ringing Cedars of Russia* book series by Vladimir Megre: This series emphasizes the importance of nature and the deep connection between humans and the natural world. It explores the idea of "Kin's Domains" and the positive impact of living in harmony with nature. These books have resonated with many readers who seek to reconnect with the Earth and appreciate the vital role of nature in our lives.

65

Uranta Loka
INNER SPACE

Inner space is so much more interesting, because outer space is so empty.

THEODORE STURGEON

Upon reaching the eighth level, the player comes to a profound realization: Everything that constitutes their material world, the reality they see and experience, is but a dream of their own creation. They are the divine observer, watching the movie of their life unfold. In this state, the player assumes the role of a conscious observer, comprehending the interplay of life, recognizing causes and effects, and witnessing processes, which brings about an incredible sense of tranquility. At this stage, it becomes clear that the chaos in one's reality is simply a product of one's own mind. Passions, emotions, life's twists and turns—all of it is a dream, and within this dream, there exists eternal silence.

On this plane of the game, the player often encounters their inner relationship with themselves. They may meet their inner child, their feminine and masculine sides, the inner controller, and other facets of their fragmented personality. It's an opportunity for the player to unite all these parts and achieve harmony within themselves. This process involves constructing their internal space, which, in turn, shapes their external world.

Much like Morpheus, the Greek god of dreams who revealed glimpses of the inner world to dreamers, on this plane of the game, the player delves into their inner world and perceives their reality as a dream. This perspective offers a deeper understanding of their own being.

Exercise: The Archetypes of Your Identity

1. Examine the feminine and masculine archetypes that shape your identity. Revisit the tales of major mythological figures, including the following:

Hestia (the unmarried aunt archetype)
Demeter (the nurturing mother archetype)
Aphrodite (the mistress archetype)
Zeus (the patriarchal god archetype)
Apollo (the favored son archetype)
Dionysus (the cared-for son archetype)
Hephaestus (the rejected son archetype)

2. Analyze whether there are any parallels in your life with these stories. Our psyche is molded by these archetypal narratives, which we enact to varying degrees.

ART THAT EVOKES THE SQUARE

- The Hero's Journey (archetypal narrative pattern): Joseph Campbell's exploration of the hero's journey archetype is found in many classic works of literature, from Homer's *The Odyssey* to J. R. R. Tolkien's *The Lord of the Rings.*

66
Ananda Loka
BLISS

> *And the idea of just wandering off to a cafe with a notebook and writing and seeing where that takes me for awhile is just bliss.*
>
> J. K. Rowling

As the player approaches Cosmic Consciousness and enters a state of pure existence, an overwhelming sense of bliss envelops them. The boundaries that separate their identity from the world dissolve, and they become one with the Cosmos. In this profound connection with the Divine, the simple acts of breathing, seeing, hearing, feeling, loving, evolving, and living are gifts in themselves. There are no longer obstacles like the serpent on this path; just two steps separate them from liberation.

The bliss experienced at this level differs from the conventional happiness derived from knowledge and action. This bliss is an innate sensation of the soul, where the player experiences true freedom and liberation, even from fear. At this stage, fear, suffering, and death are no longer reasons for concern; they are recognized as sensations and impressions within the human existence game.

In this state, individuals may feel liberated from all material concerns. The sensation is so exquisite that, at times, the player might find themselves circling between the seventh and eighth rows, repeatedly touching Cosmic Consciousness but returning to Bliss. There's a temptation to linger in this feeling, to stay within it. It is crucial, however, not to entirely dissolve into this state and to remember the purpose of their journey.

Exercise: Visualize Your World

Test your ability to visualize and shape the world around you with a single thought and the right intention. Close your eyes, visualize your purpose in this game, and imagine rolling two on the die to reach Cosmic Consciousness.

ART THAT EVOKES THE SQUARE

- *Alone in the Ocean* by Slava Kurilov: Considered one of the most remarkable adventures of the twentieth century, Slava Kurilov, a professional oceanographer, escaped from a Soviet tourist liner near the Philippines in 1974. With minimal supplies and using only a snorkel and flippers, he swam nearly one hundred kilometers (62 miles) to the Philippine coast, spending almost three days in the ocean. In his book, Kurilov details the extreme physical and spiritual challenges he faced in his pursuit of both external and internal freedom.

67
Rudra Loka
ABANDONING CONCEPTS

As far as we can discern, the sole purpose of human existence is to kindle a light in the darkness of mere being.

CARL JUNG

Why have we chosen to embark on this earthly journey? What's the purpose of our human existence? Why has life been orchestrated this way? No one finds themselves here by mere happenstance, and no life is a random error. It is in this very realm that the player attains a profound understanding of the intrinsic worth of their presence on Earth. When the soul takes on human form, it brings higher vibrations to this world. The mere act of living on this planet is an invaluable gift to the entire Universe. This realization serves as a compass guiding the player toward liberation. There is no longer a need to doubt one's existence or fret about the chosen path.

Nonetheless, this does not imply that one can act without responsibility. Each soul carries its unique responsibilities, comprising the accumulation of experiences and the elevation of its vibrations. In this realm, the player may also receive hints about their destined role in life and the particular task that holds exceptional significance for the greater good of the Universe. However, one must exercise caution, as the attachment to a role can lead to an excessive identification with it, entrapping the individual. This role might manifest as that of a parent, a child, an entrepreneur, or an educator.

This square, Rudra Loka, signifies the abandonment of concepts, identifications, and roles. The purpose of any practice is to liberate oneself from these constructs. Regardless of the path and knowledge that have guided one to this point, there comes a moment when they begin to confine rather than empower. No matter how steadfastly one has followed their path, they can relinquish it, leave behind the well-worn system they've inhabited for so long. They can carry forward the qualities and tools they've acquired, progressing freely without being bound by the system itself.

Arriving at this square serves as a reminder of the need to be the actor who plays various roles, capable of choosing a specific role as circumstances dictate. It echoes the wisdom that "to find yourself, you must lose yourself."

Exercise: Identifying Your Roles

1. Reflect on your primary role at the moment, whether it's being a parent, a professional, an educator, or something else.
2. Take a moment to identify five additional roles that you could potentially assume but may have overlooked.

ART THAT EVOKES THE SQUARE

- *Wild* by Cheryl Strayed: This memoir chronicles the author's solo hike along the Pacific Crest Trail, showcasing the idea that by losing herself in the wilderness, she found her true self.
- *The Road Less Traveled* by M. Scott Peck: This self-help book explores the journey of personal and spiritual growth, emphasizing the idea that true self-discovery often involves letting go of ego and previous beliefs.

68
Vaikuntha Loka
COSMIC CONSCIOUSNESS

The Self is not in the realm of thought. The Self is in the gap between our thoughts. The cosmic psyche whispers to us softly in the gap between our thoughts.

Deepak Chopra

Vaikuntha represents the spiritual realm beyond the confines of the material world. It is both the origin and the destination, the ultimate exit from the cosmic game. Here, one encounters the Cosmic Consciousness, the truth, the essence of all existence, and the wellspring of every manifestation. It's the state in which your desires, thoughts, words, and actions are in perfect harmony, aligning you with both your inner self and the world around you. Everything converges toward the revelation of your true nature, your path, and your innate qualities.

To be present in this realm is the player's highest aspiration, embodying divine self-awareness within human existence. In the past, reaching this state involved complete detachment from the ego, liberation from all attachments, and the remembrance of one's divine nature, ultimately merging with the world. However, in contemporary times, people tend to pursue more earthly desires. Entering Cosmic Consciousness now signifies the fulfillment of the player's deepest yearnings.

In this transcendent state, the player grasps the profound truth that karma is but a facet of the game, and that true freedom of choice transcends destiny. The soul has made a conscious decision and traversed its self-chosen path.

No work of art or exercise can tangibly capture this state. Instead, the only remaining task is to pose a question to oneself: "What game will you opt to engage in next?"

69

Brahma Loka

ABSOLUTE PLANE

The only limit to our realization of tomorrow will be our doubts of today.

FRANKLIN D. ROOSEVELT

Brahma Loka, square 69, stands as the realm of the Absolute Plane, the very inception of all existence. Here, all conceivable potentialities reside in their purest form. It's a realm of pure potential, yet it's also a place of emptiness, not the absence of everything, but the profound emptiness from which all imagination and creation are born. It's akin to the dot on a canvas, that fleeting moment between exhale and inhale. In this realm, every event, every possibility of the past, present, and future has already unfolded.

To put it simply, the Absolute Plane represents the vast variability of how all phenomena and events manifest in the Universe. It's akin to the notion of parallel realities seen in science fiction, where one world sees one set of events while another world follows a different path. There is no fixed destiny, only countless branches of probabilities.

Here, human beings feel the support of the higher forces, but the time has not yet come for their specific requests to be granted. The cosmic game has more to teach the player, and thus, the player must return to Earth. They reassure themselves, "I am not afraid. All things are possible, and I am ready to face them." They're ready to continue their journey.

It's crucial to understand that the knowledge gained at this level does not grant the right to disregard earthly and material life. In reality, anything is possible. This is the moment when humans have gained sufficient understanding and it's time to act, to manifest in life. The world awaits them, for the world truly needs them. Human life is finite. What will they do with the time they have? How will they take advantage of the opportunities that are presented to them?

As you move from one level to the next, the answers that emerge are of great significance. They will reveal why your return to Earth is essential.

Exercise: Be Mindful of Your Intentions

1. Consider questions such as the following:

   What more can I contribute?

   What do I need to reach my full potential?

What specific intention will lead me to square 72 and back to Earth?

2. Each time you roll the die, be mindful of the intention that guides you.

ART THAT EVOKES THE SQUARE

- *The Fountain* (2006): This film directed by Darren Aronofsky tells a story of love, death, and the quest for immortality, weaving elements of spirituality and interconnectedness.
- *The Tree of Life* (2011): This visually captivating film by Terrence Malick explores the interconnectedness of all life, the vastness of the Universe, and the transcendence of human existence.

70
Sattva Guna
INNER PEACE

Silence is a source of great strength.

Lao Tzu

Inner peace is a fundamental state that's difficult to describe with mere words. *Sattva guna* (also translated as "pure mind"), *rajas guna* ("active mind"), and *tamas guna* ("unconsciousness" or "deep sleep") are states that defy easy verbal expression because words belong to the realm of the mind. The best way to understand these states is to experience them.

Sattva manifests when the mind achieves complete stillness and pure awareness prevails. Think of the mind as a constantly humming computer, processing information, filtering it through its programs, and often distorting it. We find ourselves trapped in an information overload that makes it difficult to see clearly. It is only in the state of sattva that the mind finds perfect stillness or temporarily shuts down. In this state, the mind does not interfere with the acquisition of knowledge. The player at this level is connected to truth, the universal information field, or their higher self. A person simply knows. Answers flow without explanation, unadulterated by words or signs. To share this knowledge with others, it must be transformed into information, a process reserved for the next level.

Meditation, especially the kind that promotes mental stillness and detachment from thoughts, can help achieve this state. In sattva, one feels and understands without the need for analysis.

A potential pitfall for the player, however, is overidentification with the truth. The insights gained are not the result of personal merit or knowledge. Equally important is the understanding that this state cannot be maintained indefinitely. When sattva ends and the mind reactivates, the player may mistakenly convey their thoughts as the ultimate truth. They may then need to descend to lower levels, such as Violence (square 52).

In this journey, only rolling the numbers one or two will allow you to move forward. If you stay in this state for too long and find your progress stalled, consider whether you're allowing yourself the freedom to make mistakes. Are you willing to accept mistakes as opportunities for learning? For the new activity and purpose that is leading you to Earth implies an acceptance of making mistakes along the way.

Exercise: Daily Journaling Practice

1. If you find it difficult to enter the state of sattva, consider beginning a daily practice of journaling, such as Morning Pages from Julia Cameron's book *The Artist's Way*. This practice involves writing three A4 pages each morning, jotting down whatever comes to mind without judgment. You do not need to worry about grammar, spelling, or writing style because no one will read it. Initially, this daily exercise can help clear your mind of mental clutter and the incessant buzz of thoughts. By putting your thoughts on paper, you free yourself from the need to constantly chew on them.

2. In addition, when you write, you don't jump from one idea to another as easily as we often do in spoken conversation. This allows you to follow your thoughts to their logical conclusion, potentially uncovering valuable insights. A notable benefit of this practice is that once you free your working memory from intrusive thoughts, you may notice a significant improvement in your memory capacity.
3. After about two weeks of consistent practice, you may find it difficult to continue, believing that there's nothing left to write about. However, much like fasting, the initial phase involves purging everything from your system, paving the way for a detoxification process. After a month, you can reintroduce meditation, and you'll likely find it much easier to maintain focus.

ART THAT EVOKES THE SQUARE

- *The Little Prince* by Antoine de Saint-Exupéry: The Little Prince's encounters with different characters, including the Fox, reflect the simple and pure wisdom associated with sattva.
- *Siddhartha* by Hermann Hesse: This novel explores the journey of Siddhartha, who seeks spiritual enlightenment and experiences moments of sattva as he deepens his understanding of life.

71

Raja Guna

CONSCIOUSNESS IN ACTION

Action is the antidote to despair.

Joan Baez

This square, Raja Guna, represents passion and activity, a state where the mind is constantly engaged. The human mind seldom remains idle for long, especially in the context of our existence on Earth, where we must continuously process, analyze, and remember information. In the realm of Raja Guna, the mind surges with activity, as individuals strive to comprehend and organize their knowledge, attempting to integrate the wisdom they've acquired on the eighth level into a coherent system.

In this state, the imperative is to translate this knowledge into tangible information, using language, symbols, and diagrams to give it structure. Players are driven to put this newfound wisdom into practice, to test it in the real world, and for that, they need to descend to Earth. At times, this mental activity can become overwhelming, and the insatiable hunger for knowledge and experiences can lead to restlessness. Being present in the moment becomes challenging, and a sense of agitation ensues, dispersing one's energy.

Frequently, the game signals that the player's mind attempts to exert control and resist changes, discarding previous thoughts and arguments. Raja Guna embodies a balanced force of motion that propels life forward.

Exercise: Implement Your Vision

1. But where does this energy lead? It's only when you roll a one on the die that you can proceed on your journey. This number materializes when you discover the direction that demands your attention and action. Pay close attention to each roll. Reflect on the thoughts that coursed through your mind when the die revealed a one. What other issues need to be resolved now? What idea needs to be brought to life?
2. Create a detailed plan for implementing your vision, at least for the first month.

ART THAT EVOKES THE SQUARE

- *On the Road* by Jack Kerouac: This novel encapsulates the restlessness of the Beat Generation, as the characters engage in a series of adventures, seeking meaning and experience through spontaneous travel.

72
Tamas Guna
UNCONSCIOUSNESS

The darkest nights produce the brightest stars.

JOHN GREEN

To experience rebirth, you must undergo a metaphorical death, not a physical one. Here, in the game, Tamas Guna (Unconsciousness, square 72) represents the mysterious darkness that players must bravely venture into to find their way back to Earth. This stage signifies both the end and the beginning of a new phase.

Tamas Guna is typically linked to qualities like inertia, sluggishness, and restfulness. However, on the eighth level, Tamas Guna embodies completeness, density, and boundaries. At this point, thoughts are solidified and organized, preparing players to reenter the game. Tamas Guna is the energy of inertia and the serpent that guides your return to fulfill your karmic role. Inertia serves you well when you're on your own unique path. You can only descend through this serpent with focused attention and the right intentions.

As you return to The Earth (square 51), take a moment to notice: Are you repeating the same questions, or are you ready to explore something completely different? You can bring anything into the game—your projects, financial situation, relationships, spiritual path, or emotional patterns. This square doesn't mean you're starting over, but that there's still something important here. The game will guide you. Listen.

Exercise: Contemplate Your Purpose

Take a moment to contemplate the purpose or intention that guided you to this stage, and remember to carry it with you when you return to Earth. Mundane distractions have a way of sidetracking us from what truly matters.

ART THAT EVOKES THE SQUARE

- *The Little Engine That Could* by Watty Piper: This children's book emphasizes the power of positive thinking, determination, and persistence with the famous mantra, "I think I can, I think I can."
- *The Sower* by Jean-Francois Millet: This painting conveys the idea of sowing seeds with determination, a symbol of hope and growth in the face of adversity (French: *Le Semeur,* 1850, oil on canvas, Orsay Museum, Paris).

You are coming back to the square of The Earth (51) to continue your journey.

AFTERWORD

Any oracle is somewhat like the edge of a knife, which can be used to cut food or can dangerously cut oneself. Similarly, oracles conceal coveted knowledge along with dangers. Anything that, by human understanding, potentially holds answers to the most troubling questions ensnares us and our will. I've already mentioned at the beginning of the book how my uncertainty about the future and inability to make decisions independently spawned an all-consuming dependence on various "predictive tools" and practically completely atrophied my intuition. It took me great effort to get back to relying entirely on my inner voice again.

The last thing I would want is to hook my readers on this oracle, especially in a world where there are so many temptations eager to lure a person into their nets forever. Most questions that disrupt the harmony between the heart and the mind can be resolved through candid and fearless self-conversation or unbiased analysis of what's happening.

Let the question you address to the oracle be truly the one you honestly tried to find an answer to but failed, the one that disturbs the peace of your day. Then turning to the oracle will be like conversing with the Divine, conversing with a true Teacher who is capable of illuminating all the corners of your psyche and showing the way to solving the problem. There is no limit to how many times one should play this game. An infinite number, of course! But be attentive every time your hand reaches for the dice.

This book can be used not only as an interpretation of the gaming field but also as an independent guide to specific states of the psyche. You may not even play, but for several months, every morning, ask yourself, "Which aspect of my personality can I improve today? What can I change in myself today?" Trust the will of chance and your intuition and open any page. Let the book become a source of wisdom and a guide in those moments when tears, despair, anger, and sometimes uncontrollable joy cloud your clear vision of what's happening.

The interpretation of each square includes tasks or questions for reflection. I deeply wanted to move away from the contemporary model where books, internet articles, and Instagram posts offer ready-made solutions to seemingly any psychological problem one might face. Despite the archetypal structure of the human psyche, I am certain of the uniqueness of each of you and believe in your ability to sharpen your consciousness, accustomed to ready-made solutions, and return to contemplation. I have no doubt that through the combinations of squares you encounter, and the tasks presented, you will uncover certain cause-and-effect relationships in your life, shedding light on the fairness of all that unfolds and illuminating the reasons behind various events.

Life may at times seem unjust, but in the Universe, all is fundamentally fair. Nevertheless, there are many blind spots in our perception that prevent us from fully grasping the divine plan. What may seem unfair in this life is the neutralization of certain events and actions in the past. Indeed, even what people commonly call miracles or miraculous encounters are nothing more than opportunities created by the same person over centuries of incarnations and efforts.

The oracle always reveals truth, but seeing the truth is not always simple because the ego always stands guard, hiding uncomfortable truths behind seven locks, offering excuses, manipulative pretexts to postpone decision-making, and many other tricks. Do not despair and do not resist the snakes or the recurring landing on the same square; observe, analyze, feel, and inquire. Remember, this is a moment of conversation with your Teacher, a moment to ask why this is happening, how you can benefit from it for your soul.

Outside the game, this is also a highly effective rule. Do not resist people and circumstances; fully accept what is happening because resistance provokes reciprocal resistance, and aggression elicits even greater aggression from the opponent. To accept from the heart means to understand the higher purpose or reasons behind someone's behavior; when it comes to interacting with others, the game can help with all of this. How do you not resist if, for example, you are offended? Set boundaries and send to the offender, enemy, despised person, or parents whom we often condemn, a huge sphere of love (often it's not some abstract energy sphere, but a behavior, action, or reaction filled with love). With this sphere, they will have much more opportunity to escape from the dark well they find themselves in. And condemnation once again will drag both of you into the whirlpool of passions.

As written by Concordia Antarova in one of my most beloved books, *Dve Zhizn* (Two Lives):

> One must conquer by loving. If you cannot overcome the obstacle before you, lovingly, if you assess it not as a link in your own path but as the machinations of people destroying your happiness—which you also understand in your own way, wishing that neither you nor your loved ones are disturbed, and you do not recognize within yourself the higher powers to struggle calmly—days of life will be lost. And once again, somewhere and sometime, you will have to start all over again.[1*]

Use this oracle to always triumph, lovingly, and to flawlessly, easily, and with profound understanding navigate all the lessons of karma awaiting you.

---

*The above quote is my own translation of the original Russian. I am currently working on a full translation of this wonderful book.

NOTES

HISTORY OF SNAKES AND ARROWS

1. Schmidt-Madsen, *The Game of Knowledge*, 43.
2. Schlieter, *Simulating Liberation*, "Ascending the [Spiritual] Levels," 2.
3. Schmidt-Madsen, *The Game of Knowledge*, 54.
4. Lao Tzu, *Tao Te Ching*, 53.
5. Eliade, *A History of Religious Ideas*, 321.
6. Schmidt-Madsen, *The Game of Knowledge*, 148.
7. Valmiki and Menon, *The Ramayana*, 383.
8. Antarova, *Dve Zhizn*, 143.
9. Griffith trans, *Hymns of the Rigveda*, Hymn 27, Verse 17.
10. Aristotle, *Rhetoric*, 159.
11. Johari, *Leela, the Game of Self-Knowledge*, 55.

BASIC ARCHETYPES: DISSECTING THE HUMAN CONSCIOUSNESS

1. Freud, *Introductory Lectures on Psychoanalysis*, 156.

LEVEL 1: THE INNER LANDSCAPE

1. Wolynn, *It Didn't Start with You*, 145.
2. Orgler, *Alfred Adler*, 28.
3. Museo del Prado, "Table of the Seven Deadly Sins."
4. Van der Kolk, *The Body Keeps the Score*, 135.

5. Nietzsche, *Daybreak: Thoughts on the Prejudices of Morality*, 43.
6. Goldberg and Lewis, "Money Madness," 94–96.

LEVEL 6: THE JOURNEY OF SELF, NAVIGATING THE COSMIC AND THE EARTHLY

1. Rogers, *Carl Rogers on Personal Power*, 205.

LEVEL 7: DANCING BETWEEN LIGHT AND DARKNESS

1. Alex, *Søren Kierkegaard*, 73.
2. Rogers, "The Necessary and Sufficient Conditions."

AFTERWORD

1. Antarova, *Dve Zhizn*, 321. Trans, Polina Rud.

BIBLIOGRAPHY

Albee, Edward. *Who's Afraid of Virginia Woolf?* Atheneum Books, 1962.

Alex, Ben. *Søren Kierkegaard: An Authentic Life*. Northstone Publishing, 2000.

Amenabar, Alejandro, dir. *Open Your Eyes*. Sociedad General de Television (Sogetel), 1997.

Annaude, Jean-Jaques, dir. *Seven Years in Tibet*. TriStar Pictures, Inc., 1997.

Anderson, Paul Thomas, dir. *There Will Be Blood*. Paramount Vantage, 2007.

Anderson, Wes, dir. *The Royal Tenenbaums*. Touchstone Pictures, 2001.

Antarova, Concordia. *Dve Zhizni*. Uguns, 1993.

Arau, Alfonso, dir. *Like Water for Chocolate*. Miramax, 1992.

Aristotle. *Rhetoric*. Indoeuropeanpublishing Co., 2021.

Aronofsky, Darren, dir. *The Fountain*. Warner Bros. Pictures, 2006.

Aronofsky, Darren, dir. *The Whale*. A24, 2022.

Bailey, Elisabeth Tova. *The Sound of a Wild Snail Eating*. Algonquin Books, 2010.

Bender, Aimee. *The Particular Sadness of Lemon Cake*. Doubleday, 2010.

Bierce, Ambrose. *The Devil's Dictionary*. Originally published in 1911.

Bird, Brad, dir. *Ratatouille*. Pixar Animation Studios, 2007.

Bourbeau, Lise. *Your Body's Telling You: Love Yourself!; The Most Complete Book on Metaphysical Causes of Illnesses & Diseases*. BookBaby, 2014.

Burton, Tim, dir. *Big Fish*. Columbia Pictures, 2003.

Byrum, John, dir. *The Razor's Edge*. Columbia Pictures, 1984.

Campbell, Joseph. *The Hero with a Thousand Faces*. Princeton University Press, 1949.

Camus, Albert. *The Stranger*. Originally published as *L'Étranger* (Gallimard, 1942).

Caro, Niki, dir. *Whale Rider*. South Pacific Pictures, 2002.

Cooke, Lucy. *The Unexpected Truth About Animals: Brilliant Natural History, Starring Lovelorn Hippos, Stoned Sloths, Exploding Bats, and Other Wild Facts*. Basic Books, 2017.

Cronenberg, David, dir. *Crimes of the Future*. Neon, 2022.

Docter, Peter, dir. *Up*. Pixar Animation Studios, 2009.

Dostoevsky, Fyodor. *Notes from Underground*. Originally published as *Zapíski iz podpól'ya* (Epoch, 1864).

Eliade, Mircea. *A History of Religious Ideas Volume 1: From the Stone Age to the Eleusinian Mysteries*. The University of Chicago Press, 2014.

Eliade, Mircea. *The Encyclopedia of Religion: Volume 13*. Macmillan, 1987.

Fincher, David, dir. *Fight Club*. 20th Century Fox, 1999.

Fitzgerald, F. Scott. *The Great Gatsby*. Scribner, 1925.

Frank, Anne. *The Diary of Anne Frank*. Pendulum Press, 1979.

Freud, Sigmund. *Introductory Lectures on Psychoanalysis*. Hogarth, 1959. Originally published in 1917.

Fricke, Ron, dir. *Samsara*. Oscilloscope Laboratories, 2011.

Frost, Robert. "The Road Not Taken." *Atlantic Monthly*, August 1915. Also published in the collection *Mountain Interval* (Henry Holt, 1916).

George, Terry, dir. *Hotel Rwanda*. United Artists, 2004.

Gerwig, Greta, dir. *Lady Bird*. A24, 2017.

Gibran, Kahlil. *The Prophet*. Alfred A. Knopf, 1923.

Gilman, Charlotte Perkins. "The Yellow Wallpaper." Originally published in 1892.

Goldberg, Herb, and Robert T. Lewis. "Money Madness: The Psychology of Saving, Spending, Loving, and Hating Money." *Business Horizons* 21, no. 5: 94–96.

Golding, William. *Lord of the Flies*. Faber and Faber, 1954.

Griffith, Ralph T. H., trans. *The Hymns of the Rigveda*, Book 10, Hymn 27. E.J. Lazarus and Co., 1896.

Haines, Randa, dir. *The Doctor*. Touchstone Pictures, 1991.

Hancock, John Lee, dir. *The Blind Side*. Warner Bros. Pictures, 2009.

Harron, Mary, dir. *American Psycho*. Lions Gate Films, 2000.

Hesse, Hermann. *Journey to the East*. Originally published as *Die Morgenlandfahrt* (Samuel Fischer, 1932).

Hesse, Hermann. *Siddhartha*. Originally published in German in 1922.

Hosseini, Khaled. *The Kite Runner*. Riverhead Books, 2003.

Hugo, Victor. *Les Misérables*. Originally published in 1862.

Huxley, Aldous. *Brave New World*. Chatto & Windus, 1932.

Johari, Harish. *Leela, the Game of Self-Knowledge: Commentaries*. Coward, McCann & Geoghegan, 1975.

Kafka, Franz. *The Metamorphosis*. Translated by Stanley Corngold. Schocken Books, 1996.

Kaufman, Charlie, dir. *I'm Thinking of Ending Things*. Likely Story, 2020.

Kelly, Richard, dir. *Donnie Darko*. Flower Films, 2001.

Kerouac, Jack. *On the Road*. Viking Press, 1957.

Kim, Ki-duk, dir. *Spring, Summer, Fall, Winter . . . and Spring*. Sony Pictures Classics, 2003.

Kurilov, Slava. *Alone in the Ocean*. PALOMA Publications, 2016.

Lamorisse, Albert, dir. *The Red Balloon*. Films Montsouris, 1956.

Lao Tzu. *Tao Te Ching*. Penguin Books, 1963.

Leder, Mimi, dir. *Pay It Forward*. Warner Bros. Pictures, 2000.

Lee, Harper. *To Kill a Mockingbird*. Althouse Press.

Lester, Mark L., dir. *Firestarter*. Universal Pictures, 1984.

Linklater, Richard, dir. *Waking Life*. Fox Searchlight Pictures, 2001.

Lonergan, Kenneth, dir. *Manchester by the Sea*. Amazon Studios, 2016.

Malick, Terrence, dir. *The Tree of Life*. Fox Searchlight Pictures, 2011.

Manne, Joy. *Family Constellations: A Practical Guide to Uncovering the Origins of Family Conflict*. North Atlantic Books, 2009.

Martel, Yann. *Life of Pi*. Mariner Books Classics, 2003.

Maugham, W. Somerset. *The Razor's Edge*. Doubleday, Doran, 1944.

Megre, Vladimir. *The Ringing Cedars of Russia* series. 2nd edition, full set. Ringing Cedars Press, 2008.

Mendes, Sam, dir. *American Beauty*. DreamWorks Pictures, 1999.

Nietzsche, Friedrich. *Daybreak: Thoughts on the Prejudices of Morality*. Edited by Maudemarie Clark and Brian Leiter. Translated by R.J. Hollingdale. Cambridge University Press, 1997.

Noyce, Phillip, dir. *The Giver*. The Weinstein Company, 2014.

Orgler, Hertha. *Alfred Adler, the Man and His Work: Triumph over the Inferiority Complex*. Sidgwick and Jackson, 1973.

Ovid. *Metamorphoses*. Translated by A. D. Melville. Oxford University Press, 1986.

Palahniuk, Chuck. *Fight Club*. W. W. Norton, 1996.

Peck, M. Scott. *The Road Less Traveled: A New Psychology of Love, Traditional Values, and Spiritual Growth*. Simon & Schuster, 1978.

Pessoa, Fernando. *The Book of Disquiet*. Translated by Richard Zenith. Penguin Classics, 2002.

Piper, Watty. *The Little Engine That Could*. Grosset & Dunlap, 1930.

Plath, Sylvia. *The Bell Jar*. Harper & Row, 1963.

Redfield, James. *The Celestine Prophecy*. Warner Books, 1993.

Redford, Robert, dir. *Ordinary People*. Paramount Pictures, 1980.

Rogers, Carl. *Carl Rogers on Personal Power: Inner Strength and Its Revolutionary Impact*. Constable, 1978.

Rogers, Carl. "The Necessary and Sufficient Conditions of Therapeutic Personality Change." *Journal of Consulting Psychology* 21, no. 2: 95–103.

Rumi. *Rumi: In the Arms of the Beloved*. Translated by Jonathan Star. TarcherPerigree, 2008.

Ruppert, Franz. *Splits in the Soul: Integrating Traumatic Experiences*. Green Balloon Publishing, 2011.

Russell, David O., dir. *Silver Linings Playbook*. The Weinstein Company, 2012.

Sabato, Ernesto. *The Tunnel*. Originally published as *El Túnel* (Editorial Sur, 1948).

Sacks, Oliver. *Awakenings*. Harper & Row, 1973.

Saint-Exupéry, Antoine de. *The Little Prince*. Reynal & Hitchcock, 1943. Originally published as *Le Petit Prince*.

Salinger, J. D. *The Catcher in the Rye*. Little, Brown, 1951.

Salva, Victor, dir. *Peaceful Warrior*. Lionsgate Films, 2006.

Saramago, José. *Blindness*. Translated by Giovanni Pontiero. Harcourt Brace, 1997. Originally published as *Ensaio sobre a cegueira*.

Schenkman, Richard, dir. *The Man from Earth*. Falling Sky Entertainment, 2007.

Shi, Domee, dir. *Turning Red*. Pixar Animation Studios, 2022.

Soderbergh, Steven, dir. *Erin Brockovich*. Universal Pictures, 2000.

Stein, Garth. *The Art of Racing in the Rain*. HarperCollins, 2008.

Strayed, Cheryl. *Wild: From Lost to Found on the Pacific Crest Trail*. Alfred A. Knopf, 2012.

Tatz, Mark, and Jody Kent. *Rebirth: The Tibetan Game of Liberation*. Rider & Company, 1978.

Valmiki. *The Ramayana: A Modern Retelling of the Great Indian Epic*. Translated by Ramesh Menon.

North Point Press, 2004.

Van der Kolk, Bessel. *The Body Keeps the Score: Brain, Mind, and Body in the Healing of Trauma*. Penguin Books, 2015.

Van Dormael, Jaco, dir. *Mr. Nobody*. Pathè, 2010.

Van Sant, Gus, dir. *Good Will Hunting*. Miramax Films, 1997.

Wachowski, Lana, and Lilly Wachowski, dirs. *Cloud Atlas*. Cloud Atlas Productions, 2012.

Weir, Peter, dir. *Dead Poets Society*. Touchstone Pictures, 1989.

Weir, Peter, dir. *The Truman Show*. Paramount Pictures, 1998.

Wenders, Wim, dir. *Wings of Desire*. Road Movies Filmproduktion, 1987.

Wharton, Edith. *The Age of Innocence*. D. Appleton, 1920.

Wimmer, Kurt, dir. *Equilibrium*. Dimension Films, 2002.

Wohlleben, Peter. *The Hidden Life of Trees: What They Feel, How They Communicate—Discoveries from a Secret World*. Greystone Books, 2015.

Wolynn, Mark. *It Didn't Start with You: How Inherited Family Trauma Shapes Who We Are and How to End the Cycle*. Vermilion, 2022.

Yanagihara, Hanya. *A Little Life*. Doubleday, 2015.